11-20-17

Ashley,

May you relentlessly pursue God's calling.

Copyright © 2014 by Tom Cairns
All rights reserved. This book or any portion thereof may not be reproduced or used in any manner whatsoever without the express written permission of the publisher except for the use of brief quotations in a book review.

Printed in the United States of America
First Printing, Feb. 2014

ISBN: 978-1-312-04936-9

*All images were personally photographed by the authors of this book and cannot be re-used without written permission of the authors.

All Systems Go:
How to Launch a Successful Job Search

By Tom Cairns

Acknowledgements....

To the people (you know who you are) who have taken a personal and professional interest in me. Many of your stories are represented here.

Contents

PROLOGUE: WHY I WROTE THIS BOOK	9
CHAPTER 1: DO WHAT YOU LOVE AND LOVE WHAT YOU DO	11
NEVER WORK A DAY IN YOUR LIFE	12
DISCOVER YOUR PASSION	13
WHAT COMES FIRST...CAREER OR JOB?	14
A WORD ABOUT CHANGING CAREERS	20
WHAT'S LOVE GOT TO DO WITH IT?	22
CHAPTER 2: MISSION POSSIBLE	25
THERE IS LIFE AFTER _____ ?	26
COMMON JOB SEARCH MISTAKES	27
KEY THINGS TO KNOW FOR MISSION POSSIBLE	35
CHAPTER 3: CREATING YOUR COMPETITIVE ADVANTAGE	43
AUTOBIOGRAPHICAL MEMORY	44
BEFORE YOU WRITE YOUR STORY	48
BRANDING YOURSELF IN A FEW SECONDS	50
ELEMENTS OF A GOOD ELEVATOR PITCH	54
MAKING A GOOD STORY GREAT	55
CHAPTER 4: HIDDEN TRUTHS FOR A SUCCESSFUL CAREER SEARCH	59
JOB SEARCH COMES DOWN TO THESE 3 THINGS	60
THE JOB SEARCH PROCESS	60
GETTING YOUR RESUME PAST THE GATEKEEPERS	63
CHAPTER 5: THE 8 ESSENTIAL INGREDIENTS OF COMPELLING RESUMES	67
WHY YOUR RESUME NEEDS A COMPELLING STORY	68
TO WRITE OR NOT TO WRITE – YOUR RESUME	69
THE RESUME RECIPE	71
THE 8 ESSENTIAL INGREDIENTS	72

CHAPTER 6: OPTIMIZING YOUR NETWORK CHANNELS — 83

- COMMON MISPERCEPTIONS ABOUT NETWORKING — 85
- USE SOCIAL MEDIA TO OPTIMIZE YOUR JOB SEARCH — 88
- YOU ARE THE CENTER OF YOUR NETWORK — 93
- NETWORKING DO'S AND DON'TS — 94
- NETWORKING WHEN YOU HAVE A JOB — 98
- THE WHO'S WHO OF NETWORKING — 99
- CHARACTERISTICS OF A GOOD NETWORKER — 102

CHAPTER 7: SELLING YOUR STORY LIKE YOUR CAREER DEPENDS ON IT — 103

- THE SELL — 104
- CONQUER YOUR FEARS — 104
- SEEKING THE OPPORTUNITY — 107
- TIPS FOR SELLING STORY — 108

CHAPTER 8: THE INTERVIEW BEFORE YOU EVEN TALK — 111

- SITTING ON "THE" COUCH — 112
- PREPARATION IS THE KEY — 113
- THE INTERVIEW PROCESS REALITY CHECK — 114
- INTERVIEWING 101 — 116
- THE MOST FREQUENTLY ASKED INTERVIEW QUESTION — 123
- BEHIND THE CURTAIN: HOW YOUR INTERVIEWER PREPARES — 124
- INTERVIEWING DO'S AND DON'TS — 125

CHAPTER 9: CAREERTOGRAPHY – MAPPING A WINNING STRATEGY — 127

- START AT THE END AND WORK BACKWARDS — 128
- ASSESSING YOUR CHANCES — 128
- MONITORING YOUR PROGRESS — 131

CHAPTER 10: CATCHING THE IDEAL CAREER SEARCH WAVE — 133

- REVIEW THE CHECKLIST — 134
- REV UP YOUR ENGINE! — 137
- YOU HAVE THE CONTROLS — 138
- DON'T FORGET TO FOLLOW UP — 139
- ALL SYSTEMS GO — 140

INDEX — 143

Prologue: Why I Wrote This Book

There are many "how to" books about job search. But, what makes this book a must read is that it cuts through the mystery and guesswork associated with job search to focus on the three most critical elements necessary to finding and landing a job: a compelling resume, a productive network and effective interviewing skills.

Throughout my 30 plus years as a human resource executive, I successfully assisted hundreds of professionals, including CEO's and the Office of the President of the United States, in achieving their career ambitions. I would like to add you to the list. My advice is practical and easy to follow. And, it will help you to achieve your desired outcome—the job you love and one that embodies your skills, goals and passions.

Let me share with you my experiences and those of others who have used these tools to land careers and jobs they love. Learn how to apply these tools so you are not overwhelmed by the process and can actually enjoy journeying to your destination.

Chapter 1

Do What You Love and Love What You Do

Choose a job you love and you will never have to work a day in your life.
- Confucius

Never Work a Day in Your Life

According to a recent Gallup Survey, less than 30% of people like their jobs. The following pages will help the 70% who hate their jobs, are uninspired, and crave their true passion and purpose.

I have a friend named Steve who is an executive vice president with a $3.5 billion dollar company. He was not always a senior executive. Like most of us, he was looking to find a job post-graduation. Steve, who is Nigerian, attended college in London, England, and while in school he worked for McDonalds, like the one where you get your favorite quarter pound hamburger.

He started at the counter and worked his way up to assistant manager. As he was about to graduate he told his boss it was time to look for a proper job. His boss asked him why he didn't consider McDonalds a proper job. Steve thought about it and decided to stay with the fast-food restaurant where he went to South Africa to help start McDonalds there. That was over twenty years ago and the job brought him to the United States. He is no longer with McDonalds but is still in food service. In fact, his next step is CEO.

Sam's story started in college as well. Sam is presently a successful Domino's Franchise owner. His family owns 16 stores in California. I met Sam when I was teaching in Oxnard, California. He graciously agreed to visit my class and share his story with a small group of graduate business students. Like Steve, Sam needed to work while attending college to help fund his education. He started delivering pizza for Domino's Pizza working his way up to assistant manager.

As Sam was about to graduate, his boss approached him about an opportunity to purchase a distressed Domino's store. As a poor college student with debt and no credit, Sam did not think he could do it. But with a persistent boss, Sam eventually agreed to purchase the store. The contract was written on a napkin with the words: "I, Sam, agree to purchase Store #...for $1,500." That was over 20 years ago. It took a lot of hard work and tenacity, but Sam never looked back. Now, 16 stores later, it is a family business with over 400 employees and 13 million in sales annually.

You may think *that's great but food service is not for me*. You are probably right—and yet, these stories are not about food service. They are about understanding that opportunity is present, though not always obvious, and when realized it can be seized. It is also about discovering your passion. I use the word *passion* because passion like opportunity; is not always obvious, but it is present in more things than we think.

This book is about pursuing your most fulfilling career, and I hope to guide you through a step by step process to finding and landing a job that best embodies your skills, goals and passions.

Discover Your Passion

My friend once asked me to state my passion. After thinking a few moments, I started rattling off all my tasks, projects, and achievements throughout my HR career along with my interests. That's fine, she said, but what is your passion? Clearly, my answer needed to dig deeper, so I started describing in detail the things I enjoyed and what I liked to do. She still wasn't satisfied: "Yes, but, what is your *passion*?!"

At this point, I was a bit frustrated and tried to figure out what she meant by passion. I knew I had passion, but for some odd reason, I was not communicating it properly. I tried a few more times but the answers just didn't fully satisfy her—or me. It was uncomfortable not being able to fully answer such a seemingly simple straightforward question.

It would be months later when I was reading *Pour Your Heart into It* by Howard Schultz, Chairman and CEO of Starbucks, that I discovered my answer. Schultz was able to encapsulate his passion in just one word. And, guess what this simple yet delicious word was. Yep, it was *coffee*. Every one of his business decisions concerning Starbucks embraced this one solitary passion for coffee. However, it was not just any coffee—it was one that was prepared from a dark roasted coffee bean.

As I thought about this, I realized that passion is more than its definition of being a strong feeling or emotion. It starts there, but it then moves far beyond that. For example, coffee beans that are dark roasted at the highest standard of excellence are just one of Starbucks's six guiding principles. True passion is more than one's feeling or emotion towards something.

I welcomed this light bulb moment. Ah hah! Behind every passion are three important elements, and without these three threads you cannot have true passion. They are:

- **Preparation**: With a passion for something, whatever it is, spend time preparing to be the best.
- **Desperation**: Be desperate (not disparate) in terms of drive, with a sense of urgency to achieve. In the case of Starbucks, the need was to form a national company.
- **Perspiration**: It takes tremendous effort to overcome the obstacles to fulfill your passion; without perspiration and endurance you will likely give up. One needs tenacity and perseverance. Passionate people do not give up.

Let's return to the million-dollar question: What's my passion? Ironically, it took a frustrating conversation and a coffee bean for me to clearly and definitely articulate my answer. My passion is people. And so, my question for you is: What's your passion? I encourage you to really think this through before responding. I'll pause while you ponder...

What Comes First...Career or Job?

Finding your passion is important because it should guide your decisions -- not in terms of finding a job but in developing a career. Many people think a *job* and *career* are the same. Greenhaus defines a career as "the pattern of work-related experiences that span the course of a person's life."[1] Those work-related experiences are represented by a series of jobs throughout a career. Consider it this way: A career is a long-term focus that includes many short-term (not duration) jobs. A job is a means to a career.

Some people, like recent college graduates, have a short-term focus and are more interested in finding a job and will worry about a career later. However, job search will become much easier if you know what you really want to pursue. This means one should start with the long-term focus on a career.

There are many ways you can determine a career path. One is through self-assessment. Most colleges and universities offer students and alumni access to various career assessment tools. One such tool is *The Strong Interest Inventory®*. It is designed for high school students, college and adults. Another tool is *Career Leader* developed by two professors from Harvard Business School.

These assessments are just two that I am familiar with but there are many others. For example, MAPP™ career test (www.assessment.com), CareerColleges.com, eLearningPlanner.com (elearningplanner.learnkey.com) and CareerPath.com (a division of CareerBuilder). Some of these will require you to register and only give you limited feedback and will ask you to pay a fee if you want more detailed information. So, choose wisely, and make sure if you pay a fee that you receive your money's worth. If you are willing to pay a fee I would recommend you use Career Leader.

Whether you are choosing a career, in the middle of your career or ending a career (retirement is a career transition), it is critical to complete a career interest assessment. In my opinion, these assessments are dynamic and so are your career choices.

Another great way to determine or assess a career path is to talk to people about their career decisions. High school and college students should take advantage of this prior to making a career decision. Individuals who are midway into their career should do this as well—especially those desiring to make a change. Of course, people in job transition need to do this as well. If you are planning on retirement and don't want to sit on the beach all day you should do this as well, especially since you have the time to do something new and different.

Who should you target for a career conversation? You should target people who are working in areas in which you have interest, might have interest, and/or have no interest. A simple question to pose is: "How did you get to where you are today?" The stories will amaze you because you will learn that no two paths are alike. There are common threads or themes, however. For example, what is common to both Steve and Sam? Albert Einstein said that necessity is the mother of all inventions, and he is right. For Steve and Sam necessity collided with opportunity and the rest is history. There are more companies that need the kind of talent you have if you will view them as an opportunity.

You are probably thinking, *sounds like a great idea but I don't know where to find people I can talk to about my career.* The answer is simple: People are everywhere; they just might not always be obvious or visible to you.

This book's Chapter 8 is dedicated to the subject of networking, but let me start by saying you could talk to a neighbor, a friend, a parent, a relative, a fellow soccer parent, a pizza delivery person (I had to get this in!), classmates, alumni, networking event, church, grocery store, social media (Facebook, LinkedIn, etc.), etc. The possibilities are limitless, and none of these cost you money—just your time and determination. It doesn't matter where you start but once you do, it will multiply like rabbits.

Let me offer an example. I was in my office at Universal Studios in California when my assistant told me there was someone named Marques on the phone for me. I did not know Marques but I accepted the call. Marques was calling from the East Coast and told me that a friend of his had told him about me and that I might be able to offer him some career advice. I knew the friend Marques was referring to, and since he had taken the initiative to track me down, I talked to him about getting started in the entertainment industry. I told him if he wanted a career in entertainment, he needed to consider moving to Los Angeles. He had to be where the action was and also be available at any moment. I realized how hard it was to pick up and move across the country with no job and few friends, but Marques thanked me and we hung up.

Marques called me a few months later to tell me he was on his way to California and would keep me posted on his job progress. A short time later, Marques landed a job with the NFL and now has his own production group. The point is that everybody knows somebody who knows somebody. Marques knew somebody who knew me. You are just one person away your somebody. That's a great start.

Letting Go

People enter job search at different stages in their career development. There is the new college graduate anxious to start a career, a mom reentering the workforce, a retiree wanting to contribute, a midlevel professional seeking to advance to a higher position, and others desiring a completely new career path.

Regardless of which stage of career development you are in, you are transitioning from something to something else, but the only something you know is the past. This means that you need to focus on the future in order for your job search to be effective. It sounds easy, but consider what might have happened if Marques had decided to stay on the East Coast.

Here's a good metaphor for the way we should approach career decisions. We are our own Tarzan—and the key is to get a running start, grab the rope, hold on, swing as hard as possible, and let go at just the right time. The key words are: let go. It's difficult to do sometimes. Some people just want to hold on. To illustrate this, I use an example from my youth.

> *I grew up in a neighborhood where you played outdoors. Most of the time we played whatever sport was in season, but we would also head to the nearby woods to build tree houses and swing from tree to tree—like Tarzan. A vine or rope would hang from a tree branch, and we would sprint towards it, grab it at the last second, and swing to the other side.*
>
> *One day, our swing crossed a small ravine. The distance from one side to the other was about 15 feet, although it seemed like 30 feet. As the neighborhood kids would take turns swinging, some failed to jump off to the other side. And so, they would swing back and simply start over.*
>
> *Others did not have enough momentum to return to the starting point, which caused them to dangle precariously (and helplessly!) over the ravine. We would try to pull them back, but they usually fell into the ravine. Thankfully, we never lost anyone to the trenches below, but we did experience a few bumps and bruises.*

It's not just about letting go that is important it is just as important to know when to let go. Cori is a great example of letting go at just the right time. Cori is a wife, a mom and a student. She was working in a job that paid well, but she was growing increasingly dissatisfied because she wanted a job that fulfilled her passion. She decided to leave. She quit cold turkey—with no job and no safety net. Initially, it felt good but then there was the reality of bills, saving for college for her kids, not to mention she was working on a second master's degree. She kept the faith. A few weeks later, a recruiter called her about an opportunity that Cori would describe as her "dream job." The recruiter found her profile on LinkedIn. Fast forward to 13 interviews later, she landed her dream job. Turns out, she had let go at the optimal time.

To be successful in your career, you need to fully commit. The best way to let go of something is to grab on to something else. This may mean you have to let go of a job you hate or letting go of a specific dream so that you can be open for different dreams. In career search, that "something else" is focusing all your time and energy on moving forward. Jack Paar, a former *Tonight Show* host said "looking back, my life seems like one long obstacle race, with me as the chief obstacle."

Getting Where You Want to Be

Moving forward does not have to be the struggle that we sometimes make it. A career as we said earlier is a series of jobs Part of looking forward is figuring out where you want to be in terms of your career. And oftentimes, getting there will come in stages. Generally, career development consists of four stages.

The first is the developmental stage, ages 0-25 where you are preparing for life and entering the workforce. The second stage is early career where people, ages 25-40, are beginning their chosen profession. The third stage is mid-career, ages 40-55, where people typically question and reassess their career choice. The fourth and last stage is late career (ages 55 to retirement).[2] I believe a fifth stage of career development is emerging as people live longer and baby boomers are retiring. Perhaps, this is the really late career, or there is more to life career. Regardless, the point is careers are becoming more dynamic. The stages are continuous, accelerating and elongating, and people will be engaging in job search more frequently.

So, one of the first steps to starting a career search is to start with a question. *If you could do anything you wanted, what would that be?*

The response may vary according to where you are in your career development.

Take college graduates, for example. Most of them will have difficulty narrowing down their choices. In fact, my experience working with college students is that they suffer from the "I am interested in a lot of things and I don't want to eliminate any possibility." The issue for this group is they don't have a lot of work experience so their choices are limited. They do have, however, potential, which means their choices can be unlimited. Sound confusing? It is. We will talk about that later.

Once you reach mid-career, the choices may increase because you have more experience and skill. However, if it is one specific function or industry you may have trouble transitioning. This group often feels trapped, hence the infamous midlife crisis.

Late in their career people are often thinking about whether they have the financial security to retire. Also, more people don't want to retire because they feel young (and are young!). This is a great opportunity to really do something you love.

Before I move on and while this is not the focus of this book, let me say something about retirement and financial security to those of you in the development, early career stage and even mid-career stage. The people in the late stage will understand what I am about to write.

I remember the first day of employment in my professional career. I was 25 and the person working in the cubicle next to me had been in his job 5 years. I couldn't imagine being in one job for 5 years, let alone retiring in 30 years. I know you know time flies, but you really only understand that when you are looking back. Trust me that you can never make up for time lost or money not saved for retirement. The future is now.

Back to the question: If you could do anything you wanted what would that be? We don't ask ourselves that question enough. Why? Hopefully, it's because we are content, but I suspect that more often than not it is because we have become comfortable. There is nothing wrong with being comfortable in a job as long as we are still challenged.

A colleague of mine once asked his boss if he could be laid off. He had a comfortable job with good pay and no real reason to want to leave, except he felt he was going nowhere. His job performance was above average so he was told *no* but he continued asking until they said yes and laid him off. When I spoke to him several months later, he told me he was still unemployed and had one regret. "What's that?" I asked. "Not leaving my job sooner," he said. He had finally gotten out of his comfort zone and was pursuing other interests.

George Elliot said it's never too late to be what you might have been. What might you have been? It's not too late—unless you are too comfortable.

A Word about Changing Careers

Sometimes the job people ultimately want will require them to change careers. Changing careers is tough, but the good news is that it is not impossible. Part of the problem is you. That's right. You. Are your skills transferrable? The other part of the problem is employers generally tend to hire people with the exact experience they are seeking. There are exceptions, of course, and it may take more time to find them, but it is possible.

As a human resource executive, I noticed that one of the toughest decisions hiring managers had was to choose between a person with direct experience and a person without direct experience but seemed to be one of the best and brightest. I remember one manager telling me she did not have time for a 'Liza Doolittle' project. It was a reference to the film "My Fair Lady" in which an uncultured woman had to learn how to become cultured—and when she did, she excelled in every way. Today it would be Sandra Bullock in the film *Miss Congeniality*.

Like many employers, we selected the candidate with the most experience, not necessarily who had the most potential. This is not uncommon in today's job market. If you identify with the person who has more talent than experience, that just means if you want to change careers, you will need to find ways to sell your transferrable skills. For example, lawyers know how to research and write. Both these skills can be applied in other career paths. The following chapters will show you how to determine and showcase your transferrable skills.

To take advantage of this you will need to develop a resume that grabs a potential employer's attention and convinces them you have transferable skills applicable to the particular position. You will then need to elaborate in an interview and demonstrate that you know there are things you will need to learn specifically for the job and that you can do it quickly and effectively according to your skill set. Hopefully, you will have a track record that will substantiate that.

Another issue you will likely face in changing careers often requires transitioning to a different industry. This is also a challenge and is the subject for another discussion later in this book. However, let me leave you with an example of how changing careers and industries can be achieved.

I worked with a student who was completing her MBA and was an Executive Manager for a large retail chain. She wanted a career in human resources and was open to staying in retail if something was available, but nothing opened. Her retail store experience included hiring and training so she had skills that were transferrable.

It took about six months but my student was able to land a job in human resources and in a different industry sector. She was hired by a non-profit organization. This in and of itself is huge, because non-profits are usually very industry-specific. They seldom hire anyone without non-profit experience. So, what made this career change possible? It was the transferrable skills and surprisingly, it came down to a specific category of her previous work history—her profit and loss (P&L) experience.

Profit and loss is the ability to understand income and expenses, and then adjust strategies and operations to changes in either in order to produce a profit. It is more than reading financial statements or reports. Not that many people have true P&L experience, and those who do, know what it takes to run a department or business.

Thinking through what you have to offer a potential employer starts with what you believe that potential employer needs. This student did not know that P&L experience would be relevant to a non-profit or that the operational nature is a transferable skill. In the seven years she had been in retail, she was able to obtain P&L experience—it's why I suggested she include it in the summary of her qualifications. The statement was "Significant P&L experience managing and leading teams consistently delivering results." Of the 455 words on her resume, these 12 words or 85 characters (which would fit in the Twitter bio) were what helped get her the job. She was excited, and so was I. Obviously, the words alone were not enough, but she was able to articulate a skill she had that a potential employer needed. It started a conversation. The employer needed to understand how an individual with this experience could help the organization. How did an executive in secondary education know anything about the value of P&L experience?

Fortunately for my student, the executive had prior private sector experience. However, what if the executive did not understand the significance of P&L experience? Would these 12 words on a resume have been wasted? Maybe or maybe not. It all comes down to relying less on promoting a job title and more on marketing one's skill as a way to solve a company's problems.

Focusing on transferable skills is especially important when making career or industry changes. Sometimes in the case of this student, you find an employer who is seeking you more than you are seeking them. It is a perfect match. The employer wins and you win. P&L is a good example of a skill that on the surface seems applicable only in the for-profit sector. However, when you peel it back, you find project management skills that are transferable and in demand. In today's job market, far too many resumes are seen only by a computer. It makes you appreciate how the ones that make it through with 12 words can make a huge difference.

What's Love Got to Do with It?

Confucius said "Choose a job you love, and you will never have to work a day in your life." He was right, but according to a 2013 Gallup Survey this is true for only 30% of people. That means 70% either don't choose wisely or believe their choices are limited.

Traditional job search will do this to you because it focuses on finding jobs. That's why in this chapter I described how discovering your real passion and purpose is possible. I explained that it doesn't matter what stage of career development you are in and that it is never too early or too late to achieve a job you love.

I showed you tools to determine with certainty the areas that interest you. I encouraged you to let go of the past and focus on the future.

As we move forward I am going to give you the most critical tools, which include the mirapoix (resume, interview and effective networking skills) you can use throughout your career journey to sustain a most fulfilling career. Looking for a job is hard work, but when you find the right one you will never work again.

Launch Checklist

Your mission—should you choose to accept it—is to review the following status checklist to determine your readiness to proceed to the next phase of job search readiness.

Mission Readiness	Go	No Go
I am ready to be one of the 30% who loves their job.		
I completed a Career Assessment		
I know my career passion and will pursue it		

If you put a checkmark in all three Go boxes, that's grand (a word I learned in Ireland). You are ready to read on. However, if you could check every Go box with the exception of the Career Assessment, I strongly recommend you complete an assessment before reading further, because it is foundational for what follows in subsequent chapters. You will be at a competitive disadvantage without it.

Chapter 2

Mission Possible

If you Google "career search advice" you will find over 300 million results. How do you muddle through all of this? What is the most important advice a job seeker needs to know? This chapter debunks the myths of the career search and simplifies the job hunt process by providing the fundamental principles that will secure the career you desire.

There is life after _____?

It was early in my career, when I read a book entitled *Transitions: Making Sense of Life's Changes* by William Bridges. Since then I have frequently used this book as a reference to help guide me through some of my life's transitions. I have also recommended and given it to friends. In fact, if you don't have a copy you should consider getting one. I found it very helpful for job transitions, although it is not a book about job search; he focuses rather on change, which is certainly part of job search. Bridges identifies three periods we go through when coping with change. They are endings, a neutral zone and ultimately the new beginning.[3] I think you can see how these relate to career and job transitions. How well you manage the transition process will affect how successful you will be with the new beginning.

For example, I recall a very painful ending to employment for someone who had worked for the same company for almost forty years. Betty (not her real name) was the personal assistant to one of the senior executives. Her company was acquired by another company, and her position and her boss's position were being eliminated. Subsequently, Betty was offered a buyout and she of course was eligible to retire should she so desire. That was not what was painful. The problem was Betty was six months short of reaching her 40th anniversary with the company. While she knew accepting the buyout made the most economic sense, she resented having to accept it and leave before achieving 40 years with the company. It was difficult watching someone come so close to a significant milestone and not achieve it. This ending was not going to be forgotten quickly, and Betty did become very bitter.

Change like this happens all the time. Betty had a new beginning that she could look forward to but she couldn't because she could not let go of the ending. She was determined to hold on, but in the end the only person that was hurt was Betty.

The loss of a job affects many things. However, assume you can afford to lose your job, at least for a short period of time (three to six months). Could this be the motivation you have needed to do something else, somewhere else? You were unable to seize the opportunity, but ironically the opportunity has now seized you, and you are now faced with the question: Is there life after

_____? (You fill in the blank.) The answer is a resounding, bellowing *YOU BET THERE IS!*

I know this to be true because I have watched many people go through the pain of losing their job—and for some, it was their dream job to eventually land on their feet, and for some, they wished it had happened sooner. True, life as they once knew it was over, but the life afterwards turned out to be much, much better. Instead of seeing a stopping point as a destination, they saw it as a beginning or opportunity. A positive mindset is crucial to creating a new path.

I met someone recently who had just returned to work after being unemployed for one year. He was in his early 30s and married with two small children. His family had become used to him being home, and it was a big adjustment when he returned to a regular job. Although he had been home for a year, he found ways to generate income. For example, he sold some things on eBay. While he was making ends meet he used it as an opportunity to change careers. It took a year, but he enjoyed himself in the process. You may have heard the saying *necessity is the mother of invention.* This means when we really need to do something we find a way to do it.

Common Job Search Mistakes

Most people are familiar with the song "We are the Champions" by Queen. It was made famous by the repeat phrase "we are the champions" we often hear played at various sporting events. Most people don't know the rest of the lyrics. For example, in the first verse are the words:

> *...And bad mistakes*
> *I've made a few*
> *I've had my share of sand*
> *Kicked in my face*
> *But I've come through*

We all make mistakes—and some big, some little. However, all mistakes have two things in common: consequences and time. We want to minimize the consequences and the time it takes to correct the mistake. The best way to minimize mistakes is to avoid them altogether.

The following are six mistakes people make when they are launching a job search, when they are in the middle of job search, and when they are at the end of their job search. There are other mistakes you can make as well but these mistakes can cost you the most time and consequences. Spend a little time reviewing these now, and you won't have to spend time later. John Wooden, the legendary UCLA basketball coach, once said "If you don't have time to do it right, when will you have time to do it over?"

Common Mistakes When Starting A Job Search

Mistake #1: Not Setting Specific Goals

Ask yourself the following three questions and give thoughtful consideration to your answers

1. Where do I want to be?
2. Where am I now?
3. How can I to get where I want to be?

Your answers will determine the amount of effort you will put in to achieving what is most important to you. According to Goal-Setting Theory, establishing difficult and specific goals will influence your intention and direct your attention. It will organize your effort, increase persistence and commitment, and affect your strategies used to accomplish tasks.[4]

Mistake #2: Not Being Organized

Tempus fugit (Latin for time flies) is a major problem in job search. There are many activities involved in job search, and if you want to make the best use of your time you need to be organized. It does not have to be complicated, but you need to keep track of your daily activities. It is as simple as creating a journal or list in Word, Excel, or email calendar where you can enter comments on what you did that day, the names of the people and companies you contacted (whether in person, phone, Skype, email, etc.), the titles of the jobs you applied for, the outcome and next steps. You could use this list to help plan your activities and then check them off as you accomplish them. Avoid the temptation to sit at your computer all day. There are 1.6 million jobs listed on Careerbuilder.com so trying to apply for all of them is impossible and unproductive. Get out of the house or apartment and meet at least one person every week for a social visit or business meeting.

The list serves another purpose as well. It is a reminder of what you have accomplished and can encourage you when you think nothing is happening.

Mistake #3: Not Targeting Companies or Hiring Managers

Where do you find the jobs that match your areas of interest? I found my first professional job by answering an employment ad in the newspaper *The Philadelphia Inquirer*. Today, most people start by searching websites like Monster, Indeed, CareerBuilder, etc. To me, this is like running with the bulls in Pamplona Spain. There is a stampede of resumes and your only goal is not being gored. People can eventually get through, but did you know that the majority of job openings are not advertised?[5]

Companies are being more selective of where they post their job vacancies, and many believe it is sufficient to only post their vacancies on their own websites. For example, Yahoo receives as many as 12,000 resumes a week, and they are not alone.[6] This makes looking for a company seem as impossible as "finding a needle in a haystack. However, you can find a needle in a haystack if you use a magnet. In job search, the magnet is the job you are seeking. That job will lead you to finding the company or organization that best matches your interests.

So, where can you go to find these companies and organizations? You can do that by searching the web. Some good sites are Hoover's Online, Yahoo Finance, Mergent Manuals, (Name Local) Area Chamber of Commerce, City and State Directories, business and technical journals, professional associations, and the list goes on.

Once you identify the name of the company or organization, you can then search their website directly. You will most likely start with their career section, but I recommend you locate the list of executives and organization chart. Once you know the names of the people and their department you can now target the hiring manager by leveraging your network.

Target Hiring Managers

Hiring managers are different than recruiters. It is not a job and not always the same person. A hiring manager is the person who has the job opening in his or her department and will make the final decision regarding who gets hired. This is typically the person who would be your direct supervisor should you get the job.

Recruiters and human resource departments are gatekeepers, and they screen and recommend candidates. They are a significant part of the hiring process, but the person who makes the final decision is typically the boss. This is the person you want to find. Kevin Donlin, Co-Director Guerrilla Job Search International offers the following ideas:

- If the Company has fewer than 250 employees, target the President, Owner, or a VP in the group that you want to work in.
- If the Company has over 250 people but less than 1,000, target the VP of the Department where you want to work.
- If the Company has over 1,000 employees, target a Director or the VP in the Division where you want to work.
- To find the person's name search the Company's website, call the Company Directory or receptionist, conduct and online search, phone a friend.
- Search for people in your network who may be connected to the target hiring manager or Company.[7]

Common Mistakes in the Middle of A Job Search

Mistake #4: Not Focusing on the 80/20 rule

Before applying for jobs, we need to be honest with ourselves when assessing our skills and experience. I recommend you adopt an 80/20 rule when evaluating job opportunities. Your skills and experiences need to match at least 80% of the job qualifications that the potential employer is seeking. If not, don't apply.

Employers do a good job of identifying the gaps between your skills and experience and their own job requirements. If it is more than 20% they will likely eliminate you from further consideration. **Most employers focus on what is missing from your experience than on what is present.** This is an important point worth repeating. Most employers focus on what you don't have than on what you do have to offer. So, you need to be mindful of this and be prepared to tell the potential employer how you intend to close the gap between your skills and experience and what is required for the job.

Consider the following example. I am sure this position has since been filled but is typical of what a recent college graduate would face. The position is for a Marketing Associate.

Qualifications

Experience & Skills Desired:

- 0 - 2 years of related work experience accompanied by an entrepreneurial spirit
- A proactive worker with excellent planning and organization, execution and delivery skills
- Ability to represent company image and vision through customer and industry events
- Excellent writing ability and verbal communication skills
- Effective communication and interpersonal skills

Education:

Bachelor's degree required[8]

Let's assume the biggest gap to close is the 0-2 years of related work experience. How do you close that gap? You close it by demonstrating the qualifications where you are the strongest, such as excellent communication skills, interpersonal skills, planning and organization. Then you can address the lack of related experience by reaching back to the projects you worked on in college that are relatable to some aspect of marketing but more importantly are entrepreneurial. That can be something as simple as building a submarine. Sounds strange but I was interviewing a college graduate for a position who belonged to a student organization where he built a submarine. He had it listed on his resume as an activity not even a project. However, for me, it closed the gap on initiative, leadership, teamwork, project management, creativity, intelligence and curiosity. What makes someone want to build a submarine in the first place perhaps, an entrepreneurial spirit?

When traveling by train in Europe you often hear it said as you are about to depart the train and step onto the platform: "mind the gap." This is a warning passengers receive to make sure they step out of the train over the gap and onto the platform without losing their balance, tripping or falling. In job search, you need to mind the gap between your experience and the experiences that employers are seeking.

Mistake #5: Blindly Following Expert Advice

I am in the business of giving job search advice—hence, the development of this book. Some may even consider it expert advice. I like to think of it as the voice of experience. I have been a student and practitioner of finding careers for a long time. It is important to understand there is no job search advice that is tried and true. It is only tried.

For example, in Mistake #1, I recommended you set goals, but there are other experts who will tell you goal setting does not work. In fact, talk to many people about how to find a job, and you will likely hear each person saying something different. Who are you going to believe? My advice is to take expert advice, from as many people as possible. Solomon writes in the Book of Proverbs "refuse good advice and watch your plans fail; take good counsel and watch them succeed." (The Message Translation).[9]

Mistake #6: Relying on Executive Recruiters

Recruiters are hired by employers for a variety of reasons ranging from identifying to evaluating job candidates. It is important to understand that a recruiter is not your representative, although he or she may present your qualifications to a potential employer. The recruiter's job is to present the best candidates for the position, and there are usually more than one. Think of recruiters as the gatekeepers.

One headhunter, Jorg Stegemann actually tells it like it is when he says "I probably will not find you a job." That's because a headhunter generally sees no more than 10 candidates and presents at least 3 or 4 to his or her client. This is known as the short list and of course only one job candidate is hired. So, you have a 33% chance of getting on the short-list but really only a 10% chance of getting the job. [10]

Common Mistakes at the End of A Job Search

Mistake #7: Not Objectively Evaluating your Job Criteria

It is not enough to know what job you want. You need to know why it is important to you. What are the factors you want to consider when evaluating a job opportunity? The factors will vary for each of us. The following are examples:

- Something new or different from your current job
- Opportunity to grow professionally
- Job title
- Job responsibilities are significant
- Location
- Salary
- Cost of living
- Close to family and friends
- Positive team dynamics
- Provides depth and builds on breadth
- Potential for exposure
- Travel
- Other

Each of these factors has a different value, so you need to prioritize them according to their importance to you. You can end up with an Excel spreadsheet, like the following sample, which you can use to help make your decision on what jobs to pursue and ultimately which job to accept.

Whether you do something as formal as this is up to you; the important thing is to have criteria for evaluating a job before accepting it.

Sample Job Decision Matrix

	Weight	Different	Opp to Grow Professionally	Job Title	Job Responsibilities are Substantial	Location	Salary	Cost of Living	Close to Family and Friends	Positive Team Dynamics	Provides Depth and Builds on Breadth	Potential for Exposure	Other	Total Score	Weighted Score
		10	10	10	10	8	9	5	5	9	8	8	1		
Job Options															
Job 1		7	5	8	9	7	8	9	3	10	10	8	1	713	82
Job 2		7	8	7	8	7	9	9	3	5	9	7	1	671	78
Job 3, etc.		10	9	10	10	7	9	9	3	7	10	7	1	787	89

Mistake #8: Failing to Nurture Your Network

Let's assume that you have finally landed the job you were seeking. (A big congratulations is in order!) It is time to get back to work, but you should also figure out how to stay in touch with the people who have helped you in your job search process. If you don't, you will quickly get caught up in the day-to-day responsibilities and ignore the one thing that got you to where you are—and that is your network.

The people in your network understand that the level of contact will be less than it was during your job search. However, you just need to have a plan and method to touch base every so often. If you don't and should you need them again they may not be as enthusiastic. In the process of job search you will find out who your friends really are and which friends will go the extra mile.

It is not that difficult to stay in contact. The first thing you need to do is make sure everyone in your network has your new contact information. Using LinkedIn is good, but I have noticed that some people in my network have changed positions and I did not receive a direct notice. You should send out emails.

Next, determine how frequently you need to contact people in your network. Also, not everyone in your network needs the same amount of contact. For example, we have close friends whom we see only once a year because they live across the country, but when we do see them it is as though we have seen each other every day. The same can be true about people in your network.

Some people are very good at staying in touch with their network. They send notes during the holidays and other significant times. It's important that you let people know what's happening in your life; it does not have to be work related. People who have a genuine interest in you want to periodically catch up. That is how you know who your friends are because they appreciate hearing from you.

The other aspect associated with abandoning your network is failing to add to it. I was guilty of this when I was working in Corporate America. I felt I had no time to spend attending networking events, especially those of my professional associations. I still do not attend enough conferences, workshops, etc. I add people to my network regularly but it would be nice to meet some of them at an event, conference, etc., that would strengthen the relationship. This is one area where I hope you do as I say and not as I do.

Lastly, staying in contact with your network keeps your network fresh and relevant. Use your network to help others.

Key Things to Know for Mission Possible

If you haven't seen the movie, *The Secretariat*, I recommend you put it on your Netflix list. To the purist, the movie does not stick to the book, upon which the story is based, nor does it always adhere to the facts. But, that's Hollywood, nevertheless. However, it is still a must-see movie. Why?

This movie is about a famous American Thoroughbred racehorse, who in 1973 became the first U.S. Triple Crown champion in 25 years. There are other lessons about life in this movie that should not go unnoticed. The movie exposes the benefits of having a dream, making a difference, finding your voice, believing in others, being unwilling to yield to adversity (stubbornness), taking calculated risks, pursuing entrepreneurship, using strategy, and of course, embracing love.

One of the critical scenes in the movie was when the owner Penny was talking to her trainer Lucien about preparing for the final race of the Triple Crown, The Belmont Stakes. The Belmont is considered "The Test of Champions" because it comes just three weeks after the Preakness and five weeks after the Kentucky Derby. By all accounts horses are tired, and The Belmont is a grueling 1.5 mile test of speed, stamina, and endurance.

Lucien told Penny that conventional wisdom was to rest the horse from the demands of the previous two races. But Lucien wanted to do the opposite. He wanted to continue their normal workout schedule and training. This was a strategic decision for this race, but it applies to things beyond horseracing.

What strategic decisions do you need to make considering your career and job search? Do you go with conventional wisdom, or take a risk. Race horses wear blinders not to limit their vision but to limit distractions and stay focused.

Job Search is Not for the Faint of Heart

A short while back, I was helping an MBA student with her job search. She had a fulltime job in the financial services sector while pursuing her degree in a related field. However, after graduation, she wanted to pursue other opportunities that were not available at her present firm. And so, she resigned. It was a bold move, but she felt if she stayed, she would become too comfortable and not pursue her real passion. Some might think this was a risky move, and they might be right. But while risky, it is not reckless. There is a difference.

Should you leave your job without another job lined up? I would say yes, but I would add not everyone should do this. I say yes because of what I wrote in Chapter One about letting go.

My dad loved the song "Take This Job and Shove It" and it is about what the title conveys. In fact, my dad sang it at his retirement party. He actually loved his job but not always the people he worked for, which is true for a lot of people. Nevertheless, there are valid reasons to stay where you are until you secure another job.

One reason for staying put until you find something else is some employers prefer stealing other companies' employees. I know it is not technically 'stealing' and more like 'hiring away', but the result is generally the same. So, it may be easier to find another job when you have a job.

Another reason is you have bills to pay. Ask yourself if you can afford to be unemployed for however long it takes to find a new job. Although the motivation might be greater to find a new job if you are unemployed, you will still need to survive somehow and be comfortable temporarily living an uncertain future.

Consider Getting Outside Your Comfort Zone

My student had carefully weighed the pros and cons of leaving her job, and she decided to make the change. The prospect of fulfilling her dream offset the fear of an uncertain future. Further, she did something else that few people do: She went global. This meant she searched for jobs not only locally or domestically—but internationally. Today's world embraces a global economy, so why should the job search be limited to the United States? This is huge since for many people relocating to another city in the same state is difficult, let alone moving to another continent. She had wanted my opinion on the matter.

I advised her to pursue it, because expanding your job search to different industries and locations opens more opportunities. You just have to count the cost and be willing to take calculated risks. Again, risk does not mean you abandon logic; what it means is you do not dismiss a potential opportunity without making thoughtful consideration. Don't automatically dismiss something that initially feels uncomfortable. The hardest thing about the job search is opening yourself up to possibilities that unnerve you. It is a small world and when it comes to job search, failing to take a risk makes your world—and opportunities—much smaller.

You want to increase your job prospects and relocating within or outside the U.S. will do just that because most job seekers are not willing to move. I know that many job seekers will say they are willing to relocate but few actually do. About 500,000 people relocate annually in the United States and of this about one-third are new hires.[11]   That's less than 1% of the U.S. workforce.

The number working or studying outside the U.S. is actually higher. According to the U.S. State Department, it is approximately 6.4 million people or 4% of the U.S. workforce.[12] In any event, there is plenty of room for one more. I know some issues with mobility are affected by a down economy, but most of it is influenced by individuals not seeking opportunities or not being willing to accept them.

I believe everyone would benefit from relocating at least once. I have moved five times throughout my career including an assignment outside the country as a U.S. Fulbright Scholar living and teaching in Ireland. I have not regretted any of our moves and have benefited personally and professionally from each.

The exposure to different cultures and people is a great learning experience and confidence builder. Nothing gets you outside your comfort zone like packing your bags and moving some place new. Oscar Wilde said "to live is the rarest thing in the world. Most people exist, that is all."

Plan Your Next Adventure—After Retirement

Boomers, Generations X, Y, Z and beyond, now is the time to begin planning for your next adventure following retirement. Don't think of retirement as a final destination; think of it as a start to a new beginning. I know some of you have a long way to go before you actually retire, but the job market will have changed by the time you get there. Here are some things I believe you should do to be "ready" for retirement and possible reentry into the job market.

1. Treat your retirement as a Career Transition.

   After the retirement party, many people want to do the things they weren't able to do a lot of while working full-time: golfing, sitting on the beach, fishing, traveling, knitting, volunteering, etc. However, just like financial planning, if you wait until you retire to start planning the aftermath, it will be too late. I'm sure you have heard some retirees tell you that they're even busier now than they were when fully employed. And, you may have asked how that was possible. But, what are they busy doing? Most people plan their finances and think that is all there is to retirement planning. Not true. Seeking a new adventure post retirement has the same feeling it did 20 or 30 years ago, except now you have a wealth of skill and experience to offer. How do you want to use it? With your expertise and abilities, you may want to pursue another career—golfing and swimming will provide a relaxing transition, or a fun hobby.

2. Assess your career interests.

It may sound strange to hear that you should assess your career interests after working 20 to 30 years. It's a long time to figure out what you want to do in life and then get good at it. However, most people who retire want to do something different from what they did before. Take a former boss of mine, for example. When he retired, he wanted to pursue a career that embraced his love of books—and so he opened a bookstore. The business failed. He then bought a hearing-aid business. It failed too. His passion was there, but his skill-set was not. It is important to match your interests with your skills to build a successful and fulfilling career for yourself. Follow my advice in Chapter 1 on assessing your interests.

3. Inventory your employment and life journey.

Reviewing your career experiences and knowledge base is not just a walk down memory lane for nostalgic purposes. You have likely had more accomplishments than you can possibly remember. Take your time recalling past responsibilities, outcomes, lessons learned, friends, and colleagues, etc. This will help you not only focus your interests to decide your next career path, but it will also help you construct a resume and bio. We will discuss this in more detail in the subsequent chapters.

Say Yes Adventurer

My wife and I once met a fashion retailer who was in the process of selling everything in his location including the plants and furniture. He and his wife had been in the business for 30 years and had decided it was time to leave—both the business and the United States. He spent a year researching Mexico and settled on a small town near Guadalajara in the State of Jalisco. It was exciting listening to him talk about this new adventure, which others would likely describe as risky.

I began this chapter by discussing the various transitions we go through in life and how we cope with change. Every transition has an end, a period of flux and a new beginning. Ultimately, change can be good if we influence it.

I showed you how to influence your job search by avoiding the mistakes others have made. I gave you tools to make your job search more satisfying and productive.

I encouraged you to consider your options and take a calculated risk when making decisions about your career. T.S. Eliot said "only those who will risk going too far can possibly find out how far one can go."

Launch Checklist

If the below checklist was a checklist for launching a rocket or airplane you would want to mark all boxes "Go" before attempting a takeoff. But this checklist is to help determine your job search readiness, so you won't crash if you don't mark "Go" in each box, right? Maybe yes or maybe no, you decide. It's why I say your mission—should you choose to accept it—is to review the following status checklist to determine your readiness to proceed to the next career job search launch phase.

Mission Readiness	Go	No Go
I set specific job search goals.		
I have a system to organize my job search efforts		
I plan to proactively target companies I am interested in		
I understand the 80/20 rule and will use it in my job search		
I will use whatever job search advice I believe will work for me		
I understand the role of executive recruiters in the job search process		
I know my job criteria and have a system to evaluate job opportunities		
I will safeguard and nurture my network.		
I will step outside my comfort zone.		

Chapter 3

Creating Your Competitive Advantage

"The menu is not the meal."
- Alan Wilson Watts

This chapter will walk you down memory lane and pull from your mental vault an array of accomplishments and achievements you can use to market your professional self. Learn how to create a compelling story that communicates confidence and conviction to potential employers.

Autobiographical Memory

Our mind has the capability to travel back in time and recall specific situations, experiences and events about our life. These episodes are stored in our autobiographical memory. So, then how do we retrieve it?

One method is through the "specification of a context or cue elaboration with which the desired information may be associated."[13] A cue elaboration is a prompt, such as words or a situation, circumstance, event, timeframe, etc. In this chapter, I will give you ways to recall significant experiences from your autobiographical memory to aid in the construct of your own compelling story.

Sources of Inspiration

One technique in storytelling is to start at the end and work backwards. Another way, and the more traditional, is to start at the beginning and work your way to the end. Wherever you start you will still need to determine where your story begins.

Think of recalling your story as making a movie of your life. There are many phases to producing a movie, but for our purposes I will separate it into three major categories. The first stage is development of the idea or the script. The second category is making/producing the film. The final category is distributing the film. So, I think it is easy for you to see that your movie has already been distributed so you can trace your steps back, or you can go to the point of original and follow the path to the end. It is up to you. However, make sure you don't miss any important developments in the story.

When I had started my professional career in human resource management I was taught to use the Fear Technique when interviewing prospective job candidates. While interviewing can be scary, the Fear Technique is not what it seems. It is based on a method of interviewing candidates, a technique developed by Richard A. Fear. You can still get his book *The Evaluation Interview: How to Probe Deeply, Get Candid Answers, and Predict the Performance of Job Candidates*. The Fear Technique started as far back as high school and then moved forward.

I believe this is a great place to start. I realize high school was not that long ago and for others, well, a little longer. In any event, whether it is a short or long trip, it is one worth taking. You don't have to remember everything that happened in high school, unless you want to, but you should focus on the things that helped shape and influence you.

I remember one day in the eleventh grade my chemistry teacher was reviewing the answers to a test we had taken. When he got to a particular question, he emphatically stated **IF YOU GOT THE ANSWER TO THIS QUESTION CORRECT YOU WILL GRADUATE COLLEGE!** I went straight to my answer sheet and with a huge sigh of relief found my answer was correct (whew!). I can't tell you how many times I relied on that random statement to help get me through some of the dark days of college. His statement gave me more confidence than I otherwise might have had. I know it took more than this one question to get through college (and his comment might not have been true for everybody), but I hung onto this placebo nonetheless. My question for you is: What circumstances and situations have contributed to where you are today? These experiences may be good or bad.

I don't want to dwell too long on my high school days because not all of it was relevant. You can probably tell by the tie in my high school yearbook what year the photo was taken. If not, let me help you. Lyndon Johnson was President and Elvis (the real Elvis) was still alive. Give up? It was 1967.

As we move from high school we serpentine through the various events of our life arriving to the present time. This time of reflection is not a race to the finish line but a stroll through the park. It is not something to be captured in 140 characters. This process is very similar to making a movie.

You are the inspiration for this story. In the 1950's, NBC broadcasted a TV show called *This is Your Life*. The show took people through their life and featured friends, family and work colleagues. It was a very popular reality TV show. I know most people think Reality TV started with *Survivor* but the truth is a version of reality shows have been around since the start of radio and TV. So, this is your life and think of it as your autobiography and the people, places, events and experiences that have significantly influenced you.

More Experiences than You can Imagine

Your story is not about nothing. Although we know from the *Seinfeld* TV series you can make a career out of doing nothing. Your story is also not about anything or something. Your story is about everything—everything that has had a significant bearing on your personal and professional development. You notice I include personal development. A lot of our personal development comes from relationships we experienced when volunteering or from jobs we had while in college. None of those experiences are what I would refer to as "throw away." Many of those experiences provided opportunities to lead and manage people.

Let me offer an example. When I was working in Miami in the early 1990's, we were interviewing for a Director of Engineering and Technical Operations. This person would be responsible for managing approximately 40 people. We had one internal candidate who had the technical skills but lacked management experience. However, he was a volunteer leader with the Boy Scouts of America. As we discussed with him his experience as a Boy Scout leader, we learned he had supervised youth and adults and had also organized and conducted trips and other activities that required strong leadership skills. While he still needed to grow as a leader he had experience we could evaluate and gauge his potential. We hired him and invested in leadership training as well.

This took place a number of years ago but the principle still holds true. Experiences gained in a non-work setting can be applicable and relevant to a work environment. For example, the same Boy Scout position requires project management, problem-solving, decision-making, conflict resolution, communication skills, planning, and the list goes on. None of the experiences outside the workplace are insignificant. They are clearly developmental, but when it comes to work experience they are a supplement to the real thing.

Let's consider for a moment stay-at-home moms who want to return to work. What professional work experience do they have to offer? A lot, in fact I am exhausted thinking about it. Most have had to manage conflict, make decisions, manage projects, problem solve, think outside the box, adapt, say no and this is without leaving the house. They have had to lead school programs, fundraise, and I could go on. These are skills any organization needs and wants. It does not matter where you get your skill, and in some instances the stakes are even higher in a home than at work.

Mind Mapping Your Experiences

If you have ever watched the TV show *The Closer* or *Major Crimes* you know they use a white board to help solve their crimes. Whenever they face a new case, they use the board to organize the information they are gathering about the case. They write on the board, place pictures, which then become a visual tool to help them understand and look for clues to solving the case. This is a version of a mind mapping process.

You can adopt the mind mapping process to help you outline your significant accomplishments, milestones, achievements in life and work. I call this mind mapping your headlines. A mind map is generally organized around a single idea. Later, you will see how you can use this process to prepare your resume, for job interviews, networking events, etc., but for now we are going to use it to help recall your story.

Mind maps are mostly structured around words, and I advise you do the same. So, what words should you use? I suggest you use the words that describe your strengths. To find out what your strengths are I recommend you take a Strengthsfinder 2.0 assessment. I know you think I am putting you through a lot of self-assessments but it's only two (this and a career assessment), and both will serve multiple purposes.

If you buy a new copy of Strengthsfinder 2.0 by the #1 *New York Times* bestselling author Tom Rath it will include access to the assessment. It will cost you less than $15 dollars. The book is good because it offers more detailed information about your strengths. Once you complete the assessment you will receive instant feedback on your top five strengths. Read the narrative and use the five words to focus your thinking on the situations that have occurred in your life and work where these strengths were developed and applied. You will be amazed about what you retrieve from your autobiographical memory. The result is the makings of a great personal and professional story.

Before You Write Your Story

In Chapter 5, I will show you how to take the ingredients in your mind map to create a compelling resume. However, first I want to build on this mind map and show you how to use this information to answer the most frequently asked interview question that most people fumble:

So, tell me about yourself?

It seems like such an easy request, and yet most job seekers have a hard time answering it. Take a moment, and pretend somebody just asked you that. What would you say in the next 30 seconds? If you're struggling with the words, it means you don't have a strong elevator pitch.

Some job seekers will groan at the thought of developing an elevator pitch. Many of them drag their feet doing any or all of the following:

1. Creating it
2. Rehearsing it
3. Delivering it

The following will show you how to create a compelling elevator pitch that will sell your professional story and land you the career you desire.

What is an Elevator Pitch?

Imagine you step into an elevator with a person who can make or break you in terms of a business opportunity. He tells you that you have until the 6th floor to sell him on the pitch. What would you say in that short amount of time?

An elevator pitch in job search is a short summary of your professional story explained as succinctly and profoundly as possible. It is similar to a movie trailer that is designed to get you to want to see the movie. Or, it is the back jacket cover on a book that is designed to peak your interest to buy and read the book. Your elevator pitch should result in people wanting to know more about you.

Some Fun Elevator Trivia

- The first written record of the existence of an elevator is 3rd century BC Greece. The Roman Coliseum had 24 elevators.
- America currently has over 700,000 elevators, average daily trips by an elevator user is 4.
- The Close Door button does not make the door close faster.
- Every three days, the total number of elevators carries the equivalent of the World's population.
- Elevator music first appeared in the 1920s to calm fearful passengers.
- Elevators are statistically the safest way to travel.

Common Misconceptions About An Elevator Pitch

- Watching the *Shark Tank* reality TV show can provide helpful tips.
- It does not matter what you say as long as you say it with passion and enthusiasm.
- You need more than one version to accommodate different audiences.
- Connecting on a personal level will make up for a lack of content.
- You don't need to practice as long as you maintain good eye contact.
- Repeating something you memorized sounds canned and rehearsed.
- Thirty seconds is not enough time to see your story in a compelling way.

Elevator Pitch 101: What's Unique About You?

Consider this: Why would someone want to hear your story? What information does he or she want to obtain? Your elevator pitch is an executive summary of you and while brief, should include all the following:

　　a. Your Personality
　　b. Your Strengths
　　c. Your Story
　　d. Your Achievements
　　e. Your Value Proposition
　　f. Your Goals

Branding Yourself in a Few Seconds

Just like any product on the market, your brand will say a lot about you and what you can do. Of course, you're not a product—but, the underlying principle is that if people could remember only one thing about you, what would you want that one thing to be? How do you want to be recognized, and how are you different from the competition?

Here's how some companies and products want you to remember them:

- UPS - What Can Brown Do For You?"
- American Airlines – Something Special in the Air
- Capital One – "What's in your wallet?"
- Red Bull – "It gives you wings"
- Enterprise – "We'll pick you up!"
- BMW – The Ultimate Driving Machine
- EA Sports – It's in the Game
- Hallmark – When you care enough to send the very best."
- Oreo Cookie – Unlock the Magic
- The Weather Channel – Bringing Weather to Life
- Special K – Laurie Komoroski

This last one is one I adopted. Laurie Komoroski was my assistant when I worked in Philadelphia. She is among the best assistants I ever had. I called her Special K because she was.

The Power of Words

Branding your professional self is about choosing and promoting the right amount of words. Sometimes, less is more. You can search the internet and find lists of **nouns, pronouns, adjectives, verbs, adverbs, conjunctions, prepositions, and interjections** that you can use to describe your personality. Below is a list of words I put together as a sample. Once your list is complete, choose five or six of the words that best describe your personality.

> brave
> idealistic loving   tense
> intelligent   modest confident cheerfulshy kind
> dependable quiet giving bold complex patient clever able
> happy   sympathetic introverted accepting   caring warm
> searching knowledgeable trustworthy responsive   adaptable calm
> observant independent friendly spontaneous silly self-conscious
> powerful self-assertive proud ingenious sentimental dignified
> helpful energetic extroverted   organized wise religious
> nervous sensible   reflective mature
> relaxed logical witty

StrengthsFinder 2.0 What makes you stand out? I constructed the following using the narrative from my Strengthsfinder feedback.

> belief   empathy
> ideation maximizer   positivity
> includer competition   strategic
> restorative responsibility consistency achiever
> analytical woo   command
> connectedness communication individualization
> discipline adaptablility   harmony
> arranger self-assurance significance focus
> intellection deliberative developer
> context learner futuristic   relator
> input activator

Lastly, avoid overused or cliché words. Among 80 million LinkedIn users, the Top 10 most overused words and phrases.[14] These are:

Overused words:

1. Extensive experience
2. Innovative
3. Motivated
4. Results-oriented
5. Dynamic
6. Proven track record
7. Team player
8. Fast-paced
9. Problem-solver
10. Entrepreneurial

Consider replacing with:

1. Expertise in (fill in the blank, software development, mergers and acquisitions, P&L, etc.)
2. Acknowledged for creating new and alternative ideas...
3. Fast learner and driven to action
4. Consistently deliver business results
5. Strong influence skills
6. Demonstrated success
7. Adapt to ever-changing situations
8. High performance culture
9. Demonstrated ability to identify and troubleshoot critical issues
10. Take on significant accountability

Create a Visual Picture and a Quick Response Code

After you found words to describe yourself, string them together using Wordle.net to create a visual picture. Here's an example of mine:

Now I am ready to put it all into a paragraph, memorize, tweet it and make a Quick Response Code:

Hi, I'm Tom Cairns but my superhero name is HR Warrior. That's because I am a strong advocate for the business and employees. Whenever there is a conflict between the two, I find a way to meet the needs of both. That's because I am a breakthrough thinker who achieves unparalleled results. I am ready to assistant you with your organizational issues, and I'll have fun doing it.

A brief word about why I believe you should consider using a Quick Response Codes (QRC) in your job search. I am sure you have seen them but you may not have known what they are or how to read them. A QRC is similar to a bar code on a product. It has information stored on it and most are using them to store text or a link to a website.

Regent, a friend of mine first introduced me to the idea of using QRC's for video messages. Here is why this is so significant and important. You meet someone for the first time and you give him or her your business card. They put it in their pocket. A few days, weeks or months later they notice the card but don't remember anything about you. However, if your card has this intriguing stamp on it they may get curious and figure out how to access it when up pops a video of your elevator pitch or LinkedIn Profile. They are visually reminded and will likely keep your card, or better yet may call you. This could happen without the QRC reminder, but with a QRC you just creatively differentiated yourself from the competition. The following are examples.

Elevator Pitch   LinkedIn Profile

Below are internet sites where you can generate a QR Code for no fee.

```
Delivr: http://delivr.com/qr-code-generator
ZXing Project – http://zxing.appspot.com/generator/
BeQRious – http://beqrious.com/generator
Qreate & Track - http://app.qreateandtrack.com/#/create/url
QR Stuff.com – http://www.qrstuff.com/
Kayawa – http://qrcode.kaywa.com/
```

Elements of a Good Elevator Pitch

You may have an elevator pitch, but you will probably be able to develop a better one. The following guidelines[15] will help you to do so.

- **Concise.** Your pitch should take no longer than 30-60 seconds.

I want to pause here for a moment because I know 30-60 seconds does not seem like enough time. So, let me illustrate. Find a watch with a minute hand or the clock on your Smartphone that can count seconds. Now take a deep breath and hold it for 1 minute.

How many of you made it past 30 seconds? Mostly everyone, I suppose, but only a few of you made it to 60 seconds. Also, wasn't the silence deafening? 30 seconds is more than enough time to be:

- ✓ **Clear.** Use language that everyone understands. Don't use fancy words thinking it will make you sound smarter.

- ✓ **Powerful.** Use words that are powerful and strong. Deliver the "Sis-Boom-Bang" to grab their attention!

- ✓ **Visual.** Use words that create a visual image in your listeners mind. This will make your message memorable.

- ✓ **Tell a Story.** A <u>short story</u>. A good story is essentially this: Someone with a problem either finds a solution or faces tragedy. Either type of story can be used to illuminate what you do.

- ✓ **Targeted.** Aimed for a specific audience. If you have target audiences that are vastly different, you might want to have a unique pitch for each.

- ✓ **Goal Oriented.** What is your desired outcome? You may have different pitches depending on different objectives.

- ✓ **Has a Hook.** This is the element that literally snags your listener's interest and makes him or her want to know more. This is the phrase or words that strike a chord in your listeners and they can't get you out of their head.

Making a Good Story Great

Prepare thoroughly. Research and write out your pitch. Edit it, and then edit it again.

Create a 15-Word Summary that captures your message in fifteen words or less?

Here is an example using the four US Presidents who are carved into Mount Rushmore in South Dakota and a brief summary of their story.

George Washington: First President of the United States and one of the Founding Fathers

Thomas Jefferson: Principal author of the Declaration of Independence (1776)

Abraham Lincoln: Preserved the Union while ending slavery and the American Civil War

Theodore Roosevelt: Exuberant personality, founder of the short-lived Progressive ("Bull Moose") Party of 1912.

Tough act to follow but I think you get the idea.

Tom Cairns: Human Resource (HR) warrior and breakthrough thinker.

- Practice delivering your pitch. Most people spend more time writing their pitch than rehearsing their delivery. Mirrors are old school. Apps are the new school. Use both and make sure you play it back. I mentioned earlier recording your elevator pitch and embedding it into a QRC. I did that with my elevator pitch and when I watched and listened to the video I was bored to tears. It sounded dull and flat. Improvement only comes with practice.

- <u>Look for opportunities to test it.</u> People on an airplane, people walking their dog, shopping, restaurants, networking events, random encounters and of course elevators. You never know where will find them.

- <u>Have some fun - sound impossible?</u> Not really. In fact, think of it as an adventure. You may even want to put your elevator pitch to music. Below is mine.

To the tune of *Don't Worry Be Happy* by Bobby McFerrin:

(Whistling)
Here's an elevator pitch I wrote,
I want you to remember it note for note.
Don't Worry, HR Warrior

In every organization, there will be some consternation
Don't Worry, Breakthrough Thinker

Whenever conflict arises, HR warrior loves surprises
Don't Worry, HR Warrior, Breakthrough Thinker

Don't Worry, HR Warrior, Breakthrough Thinker.
(Whistling)

Launch Checklist

Mission Readiness	Go	No Go
I reached deep into my autobiographical memory and recalled specific situations, experiences and events.		
I completed a Strengthsfinder 2.0 assessment		
I used the tools outlined in the chapter to create my mind map.		
I created an Elevator Pitch that communicates my passion, my capabilities and is unforgettable.		

Chapter 4

Hidden Truths for a Successful Career Search

Cook ingredients that you are used to cooking ... In other words be comfortable with the ingredients you are using.

- Bobby Flay

Job Search Comes Down to These 3 Things

In cooking, mirepoix (pronounced meer-pwah) is a combination of onions, carrots and celery and is the base for most soups, stocks, stews, and sauces.

In job search, mirepoix is a combination of a compelling resume, a productive network and interviewing like a star. There are other important aspects to job search, but these three are at the heart of the job search process. We will discuss each in more detail in subsequent chapters; for now, though, it is important to know that although every job seeker might have similar ingredients, they will NOT have your story.

Your story is the secret seasoning

Your story is what gets released into these three activities. Let that sink in. That's why we spent time in the first three chapters helping you recall and refine your story and learning how to communicate it powerfully. Your story is the secret ingredient to a great job search. It is your competitive advantage.

The Job Search Process

Life is a process. When you wake in the morning, you go through a series of activities to prepare for the day. It may include brushing your teeth, showering and dressing, etc. This is the process of getting ready for work. In addition, it might include a stop at Starbucks, reading the paper, checking emails, Facebook, etc. Whatever your morning routines they are part of a process. That process gets you to where you are to be that day.

That process includes activities that are similar and different for you and me, but the outcome is generally the same. In this process, there are core aspects that are important for each of us to achieve. In the above scenario, I would argue that clean teeth, a clean body and clean clothes are a must. Hopefully, you would agree.

Job search is a process that consists of a series of activities designed to help us find and land our most fulfilling job. It's about knowing how to best optimize that process.

The process is non-linear

We generally think of a process as a straight line (linear) progressing incrementally, systematically from point A to point B, following a series of instructions or steps. Job search is a process with a series of actions and steps that must be taken to achieve the desired end. I have given you the three most important. A resume should come before networking and networking will lead to a job interview. That is how it looks on paper and when followed produces great outcomes.

In the real world, things don't always go according to plan so you need to have a job search process that is flexible—one that will allow you to meet people today and have a phone interview tomorrow, all before your resume is completed. That's okay as long as you have thought through your story. Otherwise, you will be unprepared and hope for the best. Knowing your story allows you the flexibility to prepare for a phone interview, a meeting, etc., on a "just in time" basis.

I view a resume, networking and interviews in the job search process as points of intersection. When I lived in Washington, DC, I commuted on the Metro subway system. Anyone who has ever taken a subway knows that sometimes you need to transfer to another line to get to your destination. Those transfer points are where other lines intersect allowing commuters to get to their destination quickly and efficiently. In job search, your story runs along the entire metro line making every stop. I can travel anywhere along this line to get to my final destination which is a job and career that I am passionate about and has a purpose.

The process of elimination

Unless you grew up in the greater Philadelphia area you may not be aware of the Mummer's New Year's Day Parade. With roots traced as far back as the 17th Century, the parade airs on local television and in 2009 made a national appearance. Participants in the Mummer's Parade typically wear elaborate and colorful costumes, and dance and march while playing banjos and other instruments including saxophones, accordions, double basses, drums, glockenspiels and violins.

It is probably the most eclectic collection of instruments ever assembled. The glockenspiel, which resembles a xylophone, and the accordion, which is a small piano strapped to your chest (not really but close), must be the most uncommon instruments to be showcased in a marching band. Nevertheless, the combination of instruments and costumes make for an interesting parade and serve as a metaphor for the job search process.

Outside of the Mummer's Parade you may not see someone playing the accordion. It is safe to assume it is not that popular an instrument. However, I played the accordion as a kid. On the right side of the accordion is a keyboard (same as the piano), and on the left are buttons that are the bass and chords. It takes strength and coordination to play as you push and pull the bellows to produce the sound. It is the pushing and pulling that reminds me of job search.

The job search process is a series of pushes and pulls, expanding and contracting, converging and diverging. To be successful during this process you have to understand that job search starts with a lot of options when trying to determine exactly what you want to do. That's why we spent time in chapter one assessing your career interests.

You may think that narrowing your job interests eliminates job possibilities. Oddly, it doesn't. By narrowing your job interests you actually increase the possibilities because it allows you to focus on the areas where you have the strongest qualifications that match your true interests and passion.

Consider TV cable channels and broadcast networks like CBS, NBC, ABC and Fox. If I wanted to watch golf 24/7 I would turn to the Golf Channel. I can still watch golf on broadcast TV but only once or twice a week and not always on the same network. If I wanted to watch cooking 24/7 I would turn to the Food Network. I can still watch cooking on the network but I have to settle for a cooking segment and limited to when they are available. I think you get the point. But just in case, one last question. Do you want to be a big fish in a small pond or a small fish in a large pond?

Getting Your Resume Past the Gatekeepers

It is not easy to scores runs in baseball or goals in soccer or football. In job search it is not easy to get your resume past the gatekeepers into the hands of a hiring manager and with Automated Tracking Systems (ATS), there is a chance your resume may never even be seen by a human being before it is dismissed into the 'No' pile. This is because many companies have been able to fine-tune their job screening filters to the point where only the "perfect" candidate emerges based on key words and metrics. For example, you apply for a regional vice president position. It is something you are doing now or have done before, except your job title was a vice president. You could be rejected by the ATS that was seeking regional vice president experience simply because your existing (or past) job title did not include "regional" and was therefore not flagged in the key search tracking system.

It is quite likely you have submitted a resume and/or application online. Unless you received an automated response acknowledging receipt you probably wonder what happens to it. One company told my friend they get as many as 1.5 million resumes that often crash their system. What happens then? The truth is this: Don't trust the system. Chances are your resume may not make it through and even if it does the odds are slim to almost none that it will find its way to an actual human being.

There is good news, however. One of my major goals in writing this book is to show you how to navigate these land mines increasing the probability that your resume will get through the ATS.

First, do your best to make sure your resume truthfully matches as many of the job requirements as possible. Focus on key terms and phrases. There are a lot of resources available to assist you in doing this. For example, I found one on Squawkfox.com.[16] In the past, matching 80% of the job requirements was sufficient, but now that is not enough. You need to pay attention to the subtleties, such as job titles versus job functions as well as buzz words. I recommend you search job sites not just for jobs but also for the titles and requirements for the job function you are most interested. One site I use is indeed.com.

You can search by job function for example, information technology, finance, human resources. The search will generate a list of jobs in human resources and their corresponding job titles. The following list of job titles is the result of a search on indeed.com for human resource positions:

   Human Resource Manager
   Human Resource Generalist
   Human Resource Business Partner
   Human Resource Administrative Assistant
   HR Recruiter
   Education/Employment Specialist
   Benefits and Compensation Coordinator

This is just a sample of the titles, and based on this search I would make sure my resume contained the following words: business partner, generalist and employment. You then need to go another level and read the job requirements for the positions. Then make sure your resume includes the words and descriptions for what the potential employers are seeking. You can't include everything but you need to include the majority of that matches. In Chapter 5 you will learn more about what to include in your resume.

My preference is to avoid the electronic system by targeting someone in the organization you are applying. A friend made cold calls until he could finally speak to someone. He still had to submit his resume and application electronically, but he had someone on the inside looking for it. By speaking to someone on the inside you can also clarify the job requirements for the position before you apply; this increases the probability that your skills will match the requirements.

Most companies are aware of the ATS gauntlet, so you may find someone sympathetic to your situation and willing to help shepherd you through the process.

Trust the Process

As you enter the process of job search you need to trust it to lead you to your desired goal. No matter your entry point in job search all roads will lead you to Rome. I never fully understood that saying until traveling in Europe and parts of the Middle East. The

Romans built roads leading to and from the cities they conquered. I got to see that influence firsthand.

The pathway to job search is through your story, and the process will include your resume, networking and interviewing like a star. At times you may feel lost or that nothing is happening; that's when you need to trust the process and know that your job search activities are leading you to your desired goal.

Launch Checklist

Mission Readiness	Go	No Go
I know the three most important activities in job search.		
I understand why my story is the key to everything in job search.		
I understand I am living in a non-linear world.		
To increase my job prospects I must decrease them.		
I now know how to navigate Automated Tracking Systems.		

Chapter 5

The 8 Essential Ingredients of Compelling Resumes

"The menu is not the meal."
- Alan Wilson Watts

A mistake most people make when writing a resume is creating a chronology of their education and work experience. This chapter illustrates how to construct a resume using eight essential elements that will convey a short compelling nonfiction story to capture the imagination of potential employers.

Why Your Resume Needs a Compelling Story

Assume your resume makes it through the ATS gauntlet we just discussed. How much time do you think a recruiter will spend reviewing your resume? According to one study, only six seconds that is less time than it takes to give an elevator pitch. [17]

This means that your resume needs to perform like a top-fuel dragster. The average dragster can race a quarter of a mile in less than five seconds and reach speeds of over 300 hundred miles an hour. That's great, except the average person reads approximately five words per second or 30 words in six seconds. So with that small or large amount of time, it is important to understand that recruiters follow a certain process to review your resume. They are looking for very specific information. This information according to the same study is:

- ✓ The person's name
- ✓ Current title and Company
- ✓ Previous title and Company
- ✓ Previous position start and end dates
- ✓ Current position start and end dates
- ✓ Education

This information would be 20-25 words for me and take less than six seconds to locate on my resume. The remaining second or two the recruiter might look for keywords that match the position. In this small amount of time, and limited information the recruiter is making an initial "fit/no fit" decision.[18]

In 2011, Google announced they planned to hire 6,000 people. In one week they received 75,000 applications without the applicants knowing what jobs were available.[19] How many of those applications do you think got reviewed? If you follow the 80/20 rule we discussed in Chapter 2 you will most likely pass the six-second reviews.

I believe the six seconds show you how important it is to have a compelling resume. One, it tells your story to a potential employer. Two, it helps potential employers match your qualifications to their needs. Remember that your story is unique. No two resumes are alike, and the person whose resume best fits the needs of the employer will receive a call for an interview. It comes down to job fit. So, how can you be sure that your resume will result in an interview and that you will be the ideal job fit? The following sections will guide you in crafting a compelling resume.

To Write or Not To Write – Your Resume

I was with some colleagues who specialize in career coaching, and we were reviewing some 'before coaching' and 'after coaching' resumes. We found that even the brightest people with great experience needed help writing their resume.

Before creating your resume, you will need to decide if you will write it—or hire somebody to do it for you. I don't know the latest statistics for the number of people who have used a professional resume writing service; however, I do know if you Google "resume writing service" you will receive over 40 million responses. Also, the cost of a resume-writing service varies greatly. I've seen them as low as $50 dollars and as high as $485 for the "Ultimate Resume." Obviously, there is a need for resume writing assistance, and it is apparently a BIG business. Why is that?

Contrary to popular thought, a resume is no longer a chronological record of one's education and work experience. In fact, it is much, much more. It is rather a script of your life journey—your professional one. It must be compelling (use action words) and show results (quantifiable and measurable). It is not a job description, but rather the achievements while in that job. The key word is "achievements." You are not simply duplicating your job description—you are showing what you achieved while on the job. This becomes part of your story. Think of your resume as a short story, a movie trailer that leaves the reader wanting to see the entire movie (to read the whole resume)—without skipping certain scenes or the credits.

How many people are skilled in that kind of storytelling? Very few, that's why many turn to an expert resume writer; however, buyer beware. Like many movies, you can go over budget and be a bust at the box office. There are more examples of movies produced with modest budgets that were huge box office hits. *The Passion of the Christ* is a prime example. Keep this in mind when shopping for a resume writer.

Choosing a Resume Writer

It had been years since I had prepared a formal resume for myself. When I needed one, I thought I could easily do it because, after all, I am a human resource professional and have reviewed thousands of resumes as part of my job. I knew what a good resume looked like, so how difficult could it be to prepare my own?

I had found some resume templates on the web and started creating. I did not consider using a resume writer. Again, I am a human resource professional, and this is my business. It couldn't be too hard. And besides, I thought if I used someone, my resume would not be my own but the work of someone else—thus, it would not truly represent me.

I soon discovered that what I was doing was the equivalent of a doctor treating him or herself. You can do it yourself, but there is a good chance you might miss something. When I had finished the draft, I circulated my resume to some colleagues and solicited their input, which proved to be most helpful. Nevertheless, what helped me the most was when a colleague introduced me to someone who was also an expert on resume writing. He was a tremendous resource, and I learned that sometimes it is more insightful and fruitful to utilize somebody else's expertise.

If you decide to hire a resume writer, the following are some tips to guide your decision-making.

- *Ask for recommendations* - The person who helped me was personally recommended to me by a colleague. That meant my colleague knew me and knew this other person. He felt we would work well together—and we did.

- *Look for someone who is interested in you* – My resume writer took the time to talk to me about my personal and professional experience and aspirations—before we put pen to paper. He wanted to know more about me and asked questions, and by doing so, gathered information about me regarding things I hadn't thought to include or had never really thought through. This preliminary interview is crucial to making sure you and your resume writer are on the same page (pun intended).

- *Look for a rocket builder* – If your resume is not carefully crafted, you may not launch a good job search or you may launch but not orbit, or you may orbit but not land. Does this mean you need a certified resume writer? Maybe, or at least someone who has done this before successfully.

- *Make sure you tell your story on paper* – A resume writer is your guide, but you do all the work. The writer shows you the path, but you blaze the trail, reviewing your personal and professional experiences, accomplishments, and measurable outcomes. You will likely walk down memory lane and recall things that were important and significant to your development and growth that you forgot. It will likely be fun and painful recalling those experiences. However, at the end of the process you will have a compelling story that you can tell with passion and confidence.

- *Make sure your resume achieves results* - A resume that does not create interest (inspire phone calls or land interviews) is not working for you. This does not mean that you made a mistake hiring the resume writer; it may just mean you might be telling the wrong story.

If you are having trouble identifying credible sources, consider visiting a website called elance.com. Elance.com is a site where you can hire freelance writers. You post the job you want them to do and the next thing you know you have qualified writers bidding for your project.

The Resume Recipe

Think of your resume as your professional recipe: There is a story you want to tell, and your experiences (ingredients) will need to be mixed and prepared in the right way so that you can best serve your knowledge, skills, and abilities to prospective employers. The following will provide some insights and guidelines for figuring out the most successful recipe to make.

The 8 Essential Ingredients

In the job search process, always remember, it's about the basics.

In retail, it's location, location, location. In the job search process, it's the basics, basics, basics. So, what are the basics? Here they are:

#1: Be strategic

We learned that recruiters first look for the following six things in a resume:

- ✓ The person's name
- ✓ Current title and Company
- ✓ Previous title and Company
- ✓ Previous position start and end dates
- ✓ Current position start and end dates
- ✓ Education

Fairly simple and straightforward, but if you approach it that way you will miss an opportunity. When addressing the basics you need to be strategic. For example, let's assume that your name is a unique family name and is difficult to pronounce. I had a student once whose first name was Pattavadee but she went by Mary. Which name should she use on her resume? I would use both Pattavadee (Mary). I might also consider next to Pattavadee showing the person how to pronounce it (pronounced Pot-ah-vah-dee). This might cause them to pause and remember you. What I am saying is, don't take your name for granted or that the person reading it knows what to do. Help him or her.

What if you are a college graduate and have no real work experience? Do I toss your resume aside, or do I look somewhere else? Education is on the list so if I am a graduate without significant work experience I would add something more about my education beyond the usual grade point average, major, school name, etc. What about your educational experience was unique or different that you can draw attention to that will differentiate you from another person with the same degree? Think about it and include a few words in your resume that describe it.

One of my favorite things that people overlook is their Company—not the name of their Company but what that Company does. I did not have that problem because NBC and General Electric were well-known companies; however, there are a lot of companies of all sizes doing significant things and no one knows who they are. That's why I suggest adding a sentence that briefly describes the Company.

For example: Haber Corporation – Encino, California

Haber Corporation was established in 1977 and is a highly respected, innovative, dynamic, and multifaceted business management and Certified Public Accounting firm.

A final word about start and stop dates. What format should you use? I prefer the dates be just the year. It is easier for me to calculate. However, if you don't have much experience, a month and year format may be better for you. Whichever you choose—the point is to just be consistent.

#2: Help recruiters get to know the real you

I had a boss who once said "to know me is to love me." It was true. You have probably heard similar statements from people you know—statements like: "Once you get to know me you will like me." What they are telling you is "there is more to them than meets the eye." This is true about every human being. Once you peel back the onion, you will often find an interesting and complex person. However, you have to spend some time getting to know them. And that's great if you have time to talk to them, but for job seekers in particular, employers don't have time to get to know the "real" you before the interview.

So, how can you attract employers' attention? I say give them a glimpse into your real personality. When someone looks at your resume, what will grab their interest?

Let's face it: Most resumes are boring. They are full of facts—albeit important facts—about you and your accomplishments. But, in a world of academic degrees and job titles, your resume is not that much different from the next person applying for the same position. However, **what is different about you is your personality**. Some people try to differentiate their resume through fonts, formats, pictures, graphs, etc. That may grab a recruiter's attention initially, but it does not tell him or her anything about you except that you may have received professional (and creative) help preparing your resume.

Know exactly what you want your resume to say about you. If you were to participate in one of my job search workshops you would be asked to introduce yourself to the other participants by stating three things about yourself. Two of the statements must be true, and one statement should be a lie. It makes for an interesting exchange. I am NOT suggesting you include a lie in your resume; what I am suggesting is to think about the person who is glancing at your resume. What can you do to cause him or her to stop and take a second look?

Most resumes focus on the factual, but personality is more than adjectives—it is more about feeling. I looked at my own resume—the initial one I had written for myself—to see what stood about me, and while my credentials were impressive, my resume was, well, boring. It said nothing about the real me. Potential employers want to know the person behind the 8 ½ x 11 sheet of paper that showcases your resume.

By the way, you should also consider your profile on LinkedIn and other social networking sites.

Why do you think employers are interested in your social network sites? They are looking for the real you. Unfortunately, on Facebook, Twitter, blogs, etc., the real you is more than most people can handle. There is real, and there is unreal. You need to know the difference. However, if you take a little of that personality and sprinkle it throughout your resume and social network sites, someone might think there is more to you than meets the eye.

You can show your personality by the adjectives you use. We discussed this earlier in Chapter 3 in the Power of Words but let me recap with the following story.

My niece Jennifer emailed me a link to a YouTube video produced by Purpose Feather out of the United Kingdom.[20] It shows a blind man sitting on the sidewalk with a tin cup and a cardboard sign with "I'm blind, please help" written on it.

People are passing him without dropping money into his tin can. A young woman walks past, pauses and then turns around and walks back to the blind man. She picks up the sign and turns it over and writes on the back. While she is writing the blind man reaches out and touches her shoes. She finishes writing, places the sign next to the can and walks away without saying a word.

Within a few minutes people start dropping coins into the tin can. This continues throughout the day when the young woman returns and stands in front of the blind man. He touches her shoes and recognizes her and asks "what did you do to my sign". The woman responds, "I wrote the same but different words."

The camera focuses on the sign with the words written "It's a beautiful day and I can't see it." The video ends with Change Your Words, Change Your World.

#3: **Error free**

Spell check is not grammar check. You may have the word spelled correctly but it is the wrong word. Some common grammar mistakes are when to use me, myself or I, and it's versus its, and my all-time favorite ending a sentence with...a preposition.[21] The best way to avoid this problem is have another pair of human eyes review what you have written, and even that is not always foolproof.

I received an email from my friend Dave who was in a panic about a mistake he had just made in an email to a hiring manager. Dave wanted to tell the hiring manager that he was confident he would hit the ground running and make an immediate positive impact if hired. However, what Dave emailed was: I am **confidant** that I would hit the ground running, etc. Spell check never caught the wrong word or it is possible the computer changed the word. In any event, confidant was spelled correctly.

We decided the best way to deal with the mistake was to let the hiring manager know. So, Dave sent a follow up email pointing out that he was indeed confident and in time the hiring manager would consider him a confidant. The hiring manager never acknowledged either email...but the good news is Dave got the job.

#4: Fill in the gaps

It would not be unusual that sometime during your career you will have a "gap" in your employment. In fact, it is more likely to be the norm. This gap is any period of time between jobs where you were not employed. For example, you worked until Nov. 2008, but you weren't hired for your next job until July 2009. It doesn't matter whether it is self-imposed or involuntary, a potential employer will want to know what you did during that time. You don't always have to cover a gap on your resume, but you will need to provide an explanation sometime during the job search process. The gap I cited above can be covered in a resume by using only the years (2008 and 2009) and not the months (November 2008 and July 2009) on your resume.

Key point: You need to put something in your resume to bridge any gaps that are greater than 1 year regardless when they occurred. However, if those gaps occurred 10 or more years ago you could consider stop citing your work experience at the 10 year mark or just prior to the gap. Employers will review your entire work experience but will be more interested in recent work experience up to the past 10 years. There is no requirement that you show all 30 years of your work experience on a resume. You need to be factual and truthful when you are closing gaps.

One of the most common gaps applies to stay-at-home moms or dads. This is not so much an issue for your resume as it is addressing whether your skills are current. So whether you put Stay-at-Home Mom or a volunteer position you had, it is more important to demonstrate how your skills are still current. Ask yourself: What did you do as a stay-at-home mom or dad that continued to develop your skills. If you were running your own daycare business, what did you learn? If you volunteered for the PTA, what roles and responsibilities did you have?

What employers want to know is if you were productive with your time. It is also common for people to say that they were consulting to cover a gap. This is fine but what will make this meaningful is if you actually had some clients and accomplishments to cite. The consulting can also be work you did where you volunteered.

The key thing to remember is that everything you do is just as important, and in some instances more relevant than work experience and education. So, don't feel uncomfortable if there are employment gaps—just be prepared for the prospective employer to ask about them.

#5: Focus on the first third

A resume is generally divided into three sections as follows. Not every resume has the same items in each section.

Section 1
Name, Contact Information, Objective, Profile Summary, Skills, Accomplishments, Education, etc.
Section 2
Work Experience and Achievements to include internships
Section 3
Associations, Volunteer Activities, Certifications, Hobbies/Interests, Language, Military, References

The conventional wisdom of most resume writers is to concentrate on the first third of the first page of a resume, which covers Section 1 and maybe part of Section 2. I agree with this thinking. All the information recruiters are seeking can be found in these two areas with the exception that education might appear in Section 3 in some resumes. People with significant work experience tend to place their education later because they received their degrees 15 years previously and experience is now more important. However, you may want to consider moving it forward—especially if you are fresh out of school.

Consider the first third of a resume as your movie trailer. A movie trailer shows you parts of the film to get you interested in wanting to see it. That is the goal of a resume. You want to get people interested in inviting you in for an interview. The tricky part about movie trailers is that what interests me may not interest you so movie makers have to use a variety of techniques to try and capture your attention. An adaptation of this to a resume would be different fonts, formats, etc. I suggest you consider bolding the six things recruiters are looking for and maybe a few of the significant items. Just don't overdo it. Remember that most people don't like reading and typically scan instead, so make your resume conducive for that.

Another aspect recommended when making movie trailers is to have others watch the trailer before you release it to the general public. A trailer that is made by the person most familiar with every aspect of the film can overlook something he or she thinks is rather obvious to the viewer, when it is not. This is another reason to have others review your resume to make sure you are sending the message you really think you are sending.

One final thought. We have all seen movie trailers that were better than the actual film. These films are generally a big disappointment to the viewer and a big disappointment at the box office. A former boss taught me to under-promise and over-deliver. The same is true with your resume.

#6 Quantify everything

Companies are looking for people who achieve results. The first thing you want to avoid is listing your job responsibilities as accomplishments. In fact, you should only have one or two sentences that describe your job responsibilities. Keep in mind that your resume is NOT an extension of your job description—it is a summary of what you achieved while on the job. Everybody with your position can say the exact same thing about roles and responsibilities. What will make you stand out is to highlight your accomplishments. Put them in the form of bullet points. The mistake people make here is they fail to quantify their accomplishments.

Why should you quantify your achievements? Because without quantification your results are just rhetoric. Employers want to see tangible outcomes, and quantifying your accomplishments is one of the best ways to get your resume noticed.

You may think that some accomplishments are not quantifiable; however, think differently. Everything can be measured. You just need to come up with the appropriate measurement. Think about what the return on investment your company/organization receives as a result of your accomplishments. Below are some examples of how quantifying accomplishments makes your accomplishments much stronger.

Before Quantify (BQ): Plan product launch events with vendors and product representatives

After Quantify (AQ): Plan product launch events with vendors and product representatives, raised $6,000 in new revenue

BQ: Strategize ways to maximize sales and profitability
AQ: Strategize ways to maximize sales and profitability; exceeded monthly sales plan by 30%

BQ: Established monthly newsletter to advertise Phi Alpha Theta History Honor Society events
AQ: Established monthly newsletter to advertise Phi Alpha Theta History Honor Society events to 1000+ student members.

BQ: Implemented and achieved strategic staffing plan while collaborating with upper level management.
AQ: Implemented and achieved strategic staffing plan while collaborating with upper level management. Secured goal of 100% staffed in 90 days by partnering with local colleges.

BQ: Led Strategic Sourcing team on interim basis
AQ: Led Strategic Sourcing team on interim basis. Stabilized organization of 40 professionals delivering $40mm in cost savings.

BQ: In charge of marketing and recruiting the Teaching Site to attract new local students and growing the University enrollment.
AQ: In charge of marketing and recruiting the Teaching Site to attract new local students and growing the University enrollment by 25 new students yearly and maintaining a 70% student retention rate.

BQ: Successfully lead the Department's efforts to advance and improve performance.
AQ: Successfully lead the Department's efforts to advance and improve performance. Achieved 125% of progress goal for Q1 2008.

#7: The right amount of content

Sometimes, less can be more. When deciding what should be or not be on a resume you need to remember the purpose of the resume. It is to attract the attention of a potential employer to consider you for an interview. The key word is *attract*. Therefore, you need to make sure your resume is straightforward and showcases exactly what the employer wants to see.

Consider this. You are driving your car, and a police officer pulls you over. Your heart is racing, and you want to get on the good side of the officer. But, the officer is all business and asks for your license and registration. Nervous (or upset or annoyed), you hand over the documents and wait to tell your story, hoping to be convincing.

A resume is similar to your license and registration (but more fun!). It is a standard document that represents who you are. Recruiters are like police officers—except you WANT them to pull you over. Therefore, you need to show them your resume in a way that enables them to see the information they need. They want to know if you match the requirements for the job. So, make it easy for them. My license looks the same as yours, except for the information. The same is true about a resume.

In my experience as an HR practitioner, I eliminated job applicants from consideration if they lacked the applicable information I needed to see, or if the content did not match the qualifications for the position I was recruiting. So, ensure that your resume closely matches the requirements of the job that is posted. This means checking that it speaks to the qualifications and includes the key buzz words. It does not mean copying the requirements listed in the employer's job posting and pasting it into your resume. If the employer requires an MBA, for example, and you own one, be sure to make sure your education is prominently displayed on your resume.

My advice is to make sure your resume contains the right information and is easy for someone to spot and pull you over. It's why headings and bullets and logical organization are all ideal. In my opinion, you get attention not by running a stop sign (fonts, formats, headings, fancy links, etc.) but by knowing someone in the precinct. In other words, this means networking (*see next chapter*).

#8 Sync your resume to the job opening

You should only submit a resume for positions that employers have posted as 'open'. Avoid sending or emailing resumes to employers who do not have job openings. Even though submitting resumes to unsolicited job positions may occasionally result in a job interview, the majority of employers will discard unsolicited resumes. Always check the status of a job position before submitting your resume—otherwise, you will waste your time.

Your resume will be one of many resumes that an employer will receive. You resume will likely need to pass through an ATS screening along with hundreds of other resumes. The resumes that most closely match the requirements of the job posting will surface near the top, and the employer will read those.

Improving the chances of your resume being read is not a matter of simply being a good wordsmith. You need to carefully review the job posting or specification the employer has issued to determine whether you have the qualifications for the position and how well you match the requirements.

Remember the 80/20 rule and avoid the temptation to stretch your experiences to match 100% of the job. The most important thing is to be honest with yourself about your qualifications and ensure you are honest on your resume.

This does not mean you need to tailor your resume for every job opening. For example, the requirements for a financial analyst are similar from one company to another. You may need to tweak your resume when applying for a position, but apart from that you can be certain that your resume will not be at the bottom of the hundreds of resumes an employer receives. If you possess the qualifications, then make certain they are obvious on your resume and then submit it.

Getting your resume to the top of the stack is the first step to landing a job interview. Then the real fun begins.

The Long Way or the Short Way

We have a choice when it comes to travel. We can take the long way or the short way. The majority of times we choose the short way because we want to get there sooner rather than later. Occasionally, we choose the long way if it is cheaper. In job search you have a choice as well. Up until now, the process of applying for positions through an automated tracking system is the long way.

I am now going to tell you the short way: networking. I would venture that the majority of jobs you have had in your career have come as the result of people you know and the people they know. Some may think networking is the long way, but they are wrong.

Launch Checklist

Mission Readiness	Go	No Go
I know what I need to do to pass the 6 second test		
I will not write my resume without some professional help		
I will focus on how I can use the 8 essential ingredients to create my resume		

Chapter 6

Optimizing Your Network Channels

Brooklyn is where I primarily developed, I had an opportunity to make records and perform in clubs here and there, and I started networking with the right people in the right places.

- Busta Rhymes

The ability to network is the most terrifying aspect of the career search. I chose the quote by American rapper Busta Rhymes to demonstrate that you don't have to go outside your backyard to network. This chapter goes behind the search scenes and explains how introverts and extroverts alike can develop a network of people who will fuel one's career search. You will learn how to harness the power of social media technology to find a career.

Why You Need an Out-of-the-Blue Network

Whether you are currently employed or in transition, there is nothing more encouraging then an unexpected phone call or email from someone in your network or an executive recruiter asking you to consider a job opportunity. You might even be flattered that someone is interested in you. These surprise calls or emails immediately get your adrenaline flowing. Albeit, your interest and their interest may be short-lived once the job opportunity is described. Nevertheless, the encounter no matter how brief is a morale booster. Somebody wants YOU (your knowledge, skills, and/or abilities).

Such out-of-the-blue inquiries are not by accident. That's right; they occur because someone likely told someone about you. Recruiters rarely cold call a candidate without a referral. However, recruiters and headhunters are beginning to use social media as a source of referral. These sudden calls and emails serve as a reminder that nothing happens out of the blue. It just takes a great network—one that is robust and diverse. And fortunately, you can develop and expand it.

Job Market – True/False Reality Check

True or False: A successful job search takes 40 hours or more of search-related activities a week.

True or False: Only a handful of people know lots of people.

True or False: Companies are investing more in employee referral programs and social network sites as recruitment sources.

True or False: The vast majority of job openings are filled by word of mouth.

True or False: Over 80% of job seekers say that their network has helped with their job search.

True or False: 5% to 25% of jobs are advertised.

True or False: The length of time it takes to land a job is determined by how much money you want to make.

True or False: The average number of employee referrals is approximately equal to the number of vacancies filled by a referral.

True or False: Only 20% of people build and nurture a network.

All the answers are True. If you want to achieve your desired job search goals you need a productive network. The following pages will show you how to do that and have fun during the process.

What Exactly is a Job Search Network?

A job search network is made up of individuals, groups, and organizations, etc., that are connected to you by one or more specific type of interdependency, whose purpose is to introduce you to people who can help you and who you can help. A robust job search network is a two-way street with you giving more than taking. We will discuss more later.

Common Misperceptions About Networking

There are a few misperceptions about networking that I would like to address.

Misperception #1: You have to be an extrovert to build an effective network.

No, you don't; in fact, it can help to be an introvert. An extrovert will sell the sizzle. The introvert will sell the steak.

Misperception #2: People who are employed don't need to network.

Wrong, the fact that you are currently employed does not diminish the need to keep a dynamic network. It serves two purposes: one, you can quickly activate should your situation change, and two, (and perhaps more important) keep you tapped into the market where you can learn about new opportunities to pursue in the future.

Misperception #3: I can always make up for a bad first impression.

Maybe, but don't count on it. First impressions are the *only* impressions. Preparation can only be done in advance—so never skip that step.

Misperception #4: Building a network is complicated.

Not if you consider constructing your network like a spider making a web. The characteristics of a spider web are that it is strong, it can stretch, and it has things stick to it, it can cover a wide-area, and it is invisible to its prey. This last characteristic may seem a little dramatic to consider a potential employer prey. However, your network is designed for you to catch opportunities.

Misperception #5: I need to have a lot of people in my network.

A network is not a popularity contest. It's not the number of people that is important. What's important is the number of people who really know you. I know people who limit the number of people they follow on Twitter because they know they can't focus on everyone. So, what is the right number of people to have in your network?

In my opinion, the answer is: as many as you want. However, if you don't want them to be just names in a social network phonebook, then you need to be "connected" if you want them to really know you. There are a variety of things you could do to make that connection, such as start a blog (an easy and free one is blogger.com), a newsletter, update your social network sites, tweet and send emails. Or, you can try the old fashioned way and meet for lunch, coffee, etc. Use your imagination and go outside your comfort zone.

Networking is about relationships that can help you achieve your job search goals. It may seem self-serving. However, networking is not about taking advantage of people, but about finding people in your network who want to help you.

Misperception #6: The stack of business cards I have collected is all I need to keep track of and communicate with my network.

Business cards are great but this relates directly to Mistake #2 in this book's Chapter 2: Not Being Organized. You need to have a system in which you can regularly monitor and track your communication with the people in your network.

Misperception #7: Social media is for staying in touch with friends and family.

You need to be comfortable using social media sites for professional networking. These sites are also a source for recruiters. One of the best social networking sites is LinkedIn.com. If you are not a member you should consider joining. There is no fee, although you can pay to upgrade your account services. I personally don't do that, but you need to decide what works best for you. Read LinkedIn's account services package descriptions and see what feels most ideal.

In any event, if you have been using the tools we covered in the first five chapters, you have what you need to create a killer LinkedIn profile. An advantage for you is that LinkedIn is the world's largest professional networking website and is great for creating and managing a large segment of your network.[22]

LinkedIn also has interesting analytic and statistical tools. For example, it can tell you how many times your profile turned up in a search within the last seven days. This gives you feedback on the quality of your profile. If you are not turning up in the search that means your profile is not generating interest. Are recruiters and HR managers looking at your profile? Could it be that you have committed one or more common job search mistakes? You may want to revisit Chapter 2.

What about when you do turn up in a search but no one contacts you? In may be because people outside your network don't have access to your full profile including email unless they subscribe to a premium LinkedIn account. There's also a setting in LinkedIn that enables out-of-network people to contact you. Another may be that your profile is incomplete. You may want to revisit Chapter 2.

There are a lot of pro's and con's to various social networking sites. It is important to know that you can't just create a profile and sit back and wait. Any form of networking must be proactive if it is going to be effective. Think back to when you were in school. Would you go through your entire day without talking to students and teachers? No. Think of networking in the same way. Touch base with them and keep conversations ongoing.

Misperception #8: Networking is all about me.

Networking is as much about you helping others as it is you receiving help. Tom Cruise in the *Jerry McGuire* film said it best: "Help me help you." Before you add someone to your network you should consider these three things: 1) Am I willing to help this person if they ask me for assistance?; 2) Am I able to help to help this person if they ask me for assistance; and 3) Is this person willing and able to help me if I ask for assistance? If the answers are all yes, then this is a good person to have (or keep) in your network.

Use Social Media to Optimize Your Job Search

Each one of us has primary and secondary social networks. Our primary network is family and after that, there are numerous secondary social networks, comprised of friends, coworkers, classmates, neighbors, fellow church patrons, teammates, and so on. Some of the people are in more than one of our social networks, but typically each social network is separate and distinct. We don't mix them. Consequently, we are not maximizing the potential of our network. Our business associates are not the sole source of potential job opportunities. You are the one common thread throughout all your social networks. You can connect your networks while maintaining their own identity and purpose, and in doing so you have expanded your job search network.

It is easy to get overwhelmed and lost when it comes to social media. Frankly, there is more available than you can ever use. That's why you need a strategy when it comes to using social media for job search.

You need it for information, ideas and networking. You need it to research prospective companies, job opportunities and people, and much more. You are limited only by your ability to provide search instructions.

You should consider becoming a member of a social bookmarking site as part of your social media strategy. In fact, you may be a member of one of the more popular sites, such as Twitter, GooglePlus, Pinterest, Instagram, Digg, Vine, StumbleUpon, Yahoo Buzz or Reddit, just to name a few. These sites account for hundreds of millions of unique monthly visitors. This is important because you can gain valuable information that will assist you in your job search activities and in expanding your network.

Your social media strategy needs to include establishing a personal presence on the web. This can be as simple as creating a profile on LinkedIn. Your profile will be viewed by countless recruiters, and you may never know it. In fact, some recruiters like to go after the "passive job candidate," which means people who are not actively looking for a job and/or are currently employed. Additionally, job vacancies will be posted. On a site like LinkedIn, there is the opportunity to join groups, which is the virtual equivalent of attending a networking session. Once a member, you can contribute to group discussions.

While I have given you tools that can help you create a killer profile you can also get help from the LinkedIn Help Center or an expert. There are LinkedIn Profile Writers just as there are resume writers.

You can also start your own blog, which is simple to do. If you don't know how, there are plenty of resources on the web that can help you, such as blogger.com. This site walks you through the blog set-up process. If you don't know what to blog or tweet, then I recommend you check out Smartbrief.com.

Smartbrief is an aggregator of information. They read all the things you would like to read but don't have time or the resources to do. They choose the most important points and package it in bite size pieces and email it to you. They do this every day based on your areas of interest.

The key point is that employers are actively seeking ways to use social networking to recruit new talent. If you establish a strong web presence, you will be ahead of where the game is going.

You may also be wondering how social media connects to job search. For instance, how does Twitter help you find a job? It's a valid concern, which is why I suggested you need to develop a strategy for how you intend to use social media for job search. This is meant to give you an idea of what is out there. You need to choose what will work for you

Don't join Twitter unless you plan to tweet. Don't join Facebook unless you plan to post. Don't join LinkedIn unless you have a killer profile. Don't receive Smartbrief emails unless you read them. Don't set up a blog if you don't have anything to say. You need to commit and then be consistent.

There are not enough hours in the day to use all the social media tools available to you. One thing that helps is that if you post something on LinkedIn you can share it on Twitter and Facebook.

The bottom line is recruiters are using these sites more and more to identify potential job candidates. You can go deeper to develop your social media strategy, and there are plenty of resources to assist. One person you should take a look at is Guy Kawasaki at guykawasaki.com. Guy was the Chief Evangelist for Apple so he knows a thing or two about social media and he blogs about it. He is an aggregator and disseminator of information. Which translated means he reads more things than you and me and will tell me things he things are important and I may want to know. I consider him my social media tutor.

Creating a Strong LinkedIn Profile

LinkedIn is the world's largest professional network with well over 200 million users and growing. As a LinkedIn member you are connected to potentially millions of other professionals. It seems difficult to believe but it is true. It depends on the number of connections you have but more importantly the quality of your connections.

The people you are directly connected to are your first level connections. However, each connection has connections and they have connections and so on and so forth until you are connected to millions of other professionals. I am linked to over 13 million professionals through my first, second and third level connections. It is not unimaginable if you believe in the power of multiplication.

A recruiter may find you directly but most likely you will be found through one of your three levels of connections. Consider the following when developing your LinkedIn profile:[23]

Background Summary – include the following:

1. Your brand identity.
2. Your value proposition.
3. Your elevator pitch.
4. Your top 5 strengths. Don't just name them, explain them. Ask your connections to endorse your top skills.
5. Your name and any aliases. I was searching for someone and found 186 others with the same exact name. You can't change your name but make sure you have as many identifiers as appropriate.
6. Make sure you include a photo. It is amazing how many people do not share a photo or some who use photos that are inappropriate. LinkedIn is not Facebook. You need a businesslike photo.

How to Stand Out from the Crowd

1. Join LinkedIn groups where you can share your point of view as related to your area of expertise
2. Reorder the content in your profile to emphasize your strengths. For example, if you are a student without much work experience then lead with your education and move work experience further down.
3. Create a QR code that links to your LinkedIn profile. You can use free tools like http://www.qrcode.ie/ to generate your QR code. You can put this code on a cover letter, resume, business card, etc.
4. If someone does a Google search on you your LinkedIn profile will be among the top search results.

How to Maximize Your Social Networking

The most popular social networking sites are Facebook, Twitter LinkedIn, and YouTube. Facebook and YouTube account for over 2 billion users. While it is common for someone to be a member of more than one site, most people spend the majority of their time and effort on just one site. Where someone spends their time and effort depends on the purpose of their social networking.

If it is primarily for personal reasons, then Facebook may be the choice; if it is for business networking, then LinkedIn gets the nod and Twitter is an abbreviated version of both personal and business. YouTube adds another dimension to personal and professional networking. The focus is on entertainment but YouTube is gaining greater use as a personal and business networking site.

While the purpose of each networking site is different they each have several important things in common.

1. They each have followers and are trying to attract more followers. They hope to capture more followers by sharing common interests and information.
2. The majority of followers are exclusive to that social networking site. Although, these followers may be on other social networking sites they are in their own individual silo.
3. There is not much information sharing across platforms. This is a function of the proprietary software applications and is why you and I need to be members of more than one social networking site.

Steve Jobs once said that "you can't connect the dots looking forward; you can only connect them looking backwards. So you have to trust that the dots will somehow connect in your future."

Each of the social networking sites where you are a member or a user you need to connect. The way you connect them is through the followers and information sharing. Right now, none of these social networking sites can aggregate all your connections and followers. That might change in the future but for now all you need to do is change your mindset about how you manage your social networking. Think of these sites as part of your social networking cloud. Your followers are in this cloud but when you engage your followers or seek to attract new followers you target your messaging for the broader follower audience. To do this you need a launching pad and I would suggest you consider using LinkedIn.

LinkedIn has the functionality for you to share information across LinkedIn and Facebook and Twitter. So, you hit three of the big four. What this requires you to do is think of your LinkedIn account as a marketing channel for Brand You. It may mean you share less information. It may mean you share less personal information. However, you will be focused and in a position to take advantage of a broader communication platform.

YOU are the Center of your Network

I mentioned in Misconception #4 that you should construct your network as a spider spins a web. What I did not mention was that at the center of an active web sits a spider. In this metaphor, you are Spiderman or Spiderwoman sitting in the center of your web anticipating results from your networking efforts.

Consider **SPIDER** as an acronym representing:

Story... everybody has one but yours is unique, so take time to create it and tell it with passion!

Perseverance... networking is time consuming; it takes creativity and moves outside your comfort zone!

Integrate... your social networks, create a compelling online profile and establish a compelling professional presence; use the internet to research how to do it and then start trying.

Don't... stop networking. Ever!

Elevator Pitch... Don't leave home without one; this is your thirty seconds of undivided attention, so create a memorable moment.

Resources... There are plenty of informational and educational resources available, and the majority are free; however, don't feel uncomfortable turning to professional writers or editors for assistance.

We discussed each of these in detail in the previous chapters, and it is important to know that the spider is active in the web.

Networking Do's and Don'ts

The following do's and don'ts are not exhaustive, yet if you keep them in mind you will build a productive professional network.

Do

Be purposeful and creative about where to find contacts. I have suggested you consider people in your social networks as part of your job search network. Many times we overlook the obvious people in our life, such as family and friends as not being important to our job search. We tend to think about only professional relationships. I know a number of college graduates whose parents run a family business and want them to join them. However, not all do, which is fine except, they don't let their parents help them in their job search by being an active part of your network. This is a missed opportunity; they obviously have business contacts that could be helpful.

Join a professional association related to your field. Typically these organizations have meetings where you can attend and network. Some examples are:

- American Association of Healthcare Administrative Management
- American Management Association
- Association for Healthcare Resource & Materials Management
- Association of Information Technology Professionals
- Association of Nutrition and Food Service Professionals
- Association of Professionals in Business Management
- Financial Management Association
- Sales and Marketing Professional Association
- Society for Human Resource Management

Find and join a group on LinkedIn. You can search for "groups you may like" on LinkedIn.[24] The search will generally produce groups that align with the profile you created in LinkedIn. You will see the name of the group/organization and a brief description of the type of group it is. Many of the groups represent professional associations.

Find a mentor, be a mentor, or volunteer. Believe it or not, you benefit the most from volunteering or being a mentor. That is not the reason you do it but if you have ever mentored, you know this is true. It is especially important to keep it up if you are in job transition.

Develop a system of organizing and communicating with your contacts. We discussed this in Chapter 2 and gave examples of how you can easily do this. Think Nike, and just do it.

Conduct business blind dates. Nothing romantic here. As you begin networking you will be referred to other people. For some of those people, it would be helpful to meet them in person. I am sure you notice people meeting people for the first time at Starbucks, Corner Bakery, etc. It provides a comfortable and fun atmosphere in which to get to know each other.

Meet people. Meet more people. Call, or send e-mails, notes and cards. You will never run out of people to meet. Be selective, but keep expanding your contacts.

Attend events, learn to work the room, make people think you are likeable and interesting. Networking events keep you motivated and introduce you to other people experiencing the same thing as you. They help keep you accountable. Lastly, they are a good source of what is happening in the market and will often try to help you in your search.

Establish a social network presence. We discussed how to do this and the importance of doing it. Again think Nike and just do it.

Have a killer commercial that inspires someone to want to buy the product (invest in you). This is your elevator pitch. Revisit Chapter 3.

Help others. This is the principle of paying it forward. Sometimes the best way you can help yourself is to help someone else.

Be diligent in doing these things and you will have a productive and effective network. You will also develop close and long-lasting relationships.

Don't

Let your contacts get stale or unproductive. A spider web that is inactive is a cobweb. Keeping your network fresh and vibrant is your responsibility. If you are active in job search, make it a point to email your contacts at least monthly to update them on what is new. It does not have to always involve an update on job search. It can be your wedding anniversary or your daughter winning the State Spelling Bee. Keep this up once you have a job, but maybe do it quarterly. You may want to use your note to ask them what is new with them. Show an interest in them as well.

Join every association, group or organization; instead, be specific and targeted. While I encourage you to join professional organizations, attend networking events and become members of social networking online, you need to adopt the 'less is more' approach. Be discerning in which you choose to attend.

Discount volunteering and being a mentor. You are not only denying someone else the benefit of your volunteering or mentoring, but you are also denying yourself the benefit you gain from helping someone else. There is research that shows people who help others are "more likely to be happy and satisfied with their lives."[25]

Miss updating your journal on your activities, and schedule daily and weekly tasks. This updates your progress and serves to motivate further action. You have likely heard it said: If you fail to plan, you plan to fail.

Stop picking someone's brain. Not the best visual, but you get the point. Stay intellectually curious and you will learn a lot.

Neglect to thank your contacts with call, e-mail, notes and cards. The majority of people in your network are helping you for free, and in most cases if you had to pay them you could not afford them. A simple thank-you goes a long way and shows you don't take them for granted.

Speak without listening, or get trapped, or hang with just one person. It is easy—especially for an introvert—to find a corner with one or two people at a networking event/meeting and hang out for the day or night. One way to keep moving forward is to look for two or three others and go join them. Groups of three are the best.

Let your social network dominate you. By dominate I mean take over your life. You want to be active, but not overactive; otherwise you might hyperventilate. I gave up following some people on Twitter because not every activity in their life needed to be tweeted.

Ignore the importance of perfecting your elevator pitch. Avoid the temptation that every time someone asks you to tell them about yourself that you have to have something new to say. One of the best ways to be remembered is for everyone you meet to know the same thing about you.

Fail to help others. You have heard it said there are two types of people in the world – givers and takers. In job search you take what you give.

Networking When You Have a Job

How do you build an effective network when you have a job? And why would you even want to do so? It may be surprising to learn that most people do not network inside or outside their company. This is a lost opportunity. To take advantage of networking within your company, you must overcome the barriers to internal networking. The benefits of networking don't stop once you have a job. We discussed earlier how to keep your network fresh and not become a cobweb. Those barriers to networking while employed are:

1. **"I don't need to because I have a job."** True, but is this your forever job? As Yogi Berra once said, "The future ain't what it used to be."

2. **"I don't know who to contact."** Not true; you have access to the people in your chain of command, department, division, etc. You also have access to the one thing an outsider does not -- and that is the company organization chart, complete with phone numbers and email addresses. You also meet people at company functions i.e., training, cafeteria, town halls, business presentations, affinity groups, etc. While you have access, don't abuse it and make sure your employer does not have any policies restricting the type of contact you can have with executives and clients

3. **"I don't know what to say."** Not true; you work in the same company and as such have a lot in common. You contribute to the bottom line. Talk about the business, where it is going, how it could be improved, what is working, what is not working, ask them how they got to where they are. The dialogue is endless; you just need to know the metrics of the business.

4. **"What will my colleagues think (that I am a self-promoting brown-noser)?"** Internal networking is self-prompting, and if you don't do it then who will? I am half-serious. Internal networking is delicate, and the perception can be that you are stepping over the line. Especially if you meet with executives who are higher than your boss.. My suggestion is that you discuss your objectives with your boss and get his or her support before you go outside the chain of command. The best thing would be to have your boss refer you. As for your fellow colleagues, they can do the same thing you do.

Internal networking will help you with your career goals. Remember the majority of people do not network so this is a competitive advantage for you. Most job vacancies are filled by word-of-mouth. This applies to internal jobs and external jobs.

The Who's Who of Networking

The most popular job websites are Monster, CareerBuilder, USA.jobs, Simply Hired, Indeed.com, LinkedIn, Glassdoor, AOL find a job, and snagajob. They account for over an estimated 100,000 unique monthly visitors with Monster and CareerBuilder taking the majority.[26] What does this mean for the individual job seeker? It might represent tremendous opportunity, or it could mean the odds of landing a job through the Internet are insurmountable. The truth is the majority of jobs are filled the old-fashioned way—by who you know.

You have likely heard it said, "it is not what you know but who you know that matters." In the case of the job search, it is both. What you know is a combination of education, work, and life experience. Who you know are the people in your network.

How do you build a network? Most job seekers believe it takes a lot of time, energy, and work. The perception is you attend a bunch of networking meetings to meet people. The reality is most networking occurs one on one, which may seem even more daunting. How do you meet people you need to know if you do not know them?

The most straightforward way to start is with the people in your social networks we described earlier: your family, friends, students/colleagues, alumni, professional associations and recruiters/search firms. These represent your six degrees of separation from you and the job you want. Your message should be clear and concise. You are seeking knowledge about the job market and your corresponding interests.

What most job seekers do not realize is that potential employers are doing something similar. Whenever they have a job vacancy, they first network with the people they know who are colleagues, friends in the business, alumni, professional associations, and recruiters/search firms. What you as a job seeker want is for your network to intersect with the network of a potential employer. This is when opportunity meets availability and hopefully leads to employability. As a general rule of thumb, you should have at least 100 people in your network. Obviously, the quality of your network is more important than the number.

The Internet can assist you in finding friends, alumni, colleagues, associations, recruiters, etc.

An example of working your network

"You're brilliant, we're hiring." This was the job ad posted by Google—and it grabbed the attention of Minnie Ingersoll's mom. She told her daughter and yada yada, so on and so forth, and now Minnie is a Product Manager at Google.

Sounds easy, but is that all it took? Yes, if you are Google. However, what about Minnie, and how did her resume rise to the top? For one, she was brilliant, or at least her mom thought so and, apparently, now Google. But, what may have helped the most was that she leveraged her experience as a Stanford computer science graduate to network with former classmates who were employed at Google. BINGO! The majority of jobs are filled by word-of-mouth.

Oh, the power and influence of alumni. Any idea how many Stanford graduates are employed by Google? I was unable to find the exact number, but I did learn that Google targets Stanford Computer Science graduates. No surprise.

There is nothing wrong with a company hiring graduates from the school where the CEO or other senior executives have graduated. In fact, it is quite common. Success breeds success, and familiarity also breeds familiarity. You tend to go with who you know and what you know. This means you should take advantage of your alumni associations. They can be more beneficial to your job search than you think. Most people avoid their alumni association because they think it is about fundraising. However, most alumni are proud of their college/university and whenever they meet fellow alumni are more than happy to talk about their experience while at school no matter how long ago they graduated. If you want to know how to connect with the alumni association for your college/university simply contact the Office of Advancement and they will point you in the right direction. While you are doing this you may also want to consider your high school alumni association as well. If it ends up costing you a small donation it might prove to be a wise investment.

Your mission as a prospective job candidate is to get known. Minnie leveraged the one factor in her background that could get her known. It was a fairly significant factor, but that was all she needed to get in the door. In 2009, Southwest Airlines received over 90,000 resumes, and they hired less than 1,000 people. That is a 90 to 1 ratio. I can only imagine what the ratio must be for other companies like Google.

Minnie beat the odds—and so can you. Minnie looked inside the organization to identify someone who could provide her insight into the company and perhaps even a referral or personal recommendation You can do the same. It may be a college affiliation or perhaps a former colleague from a company where you worked or volunteered. What you need to do is determine how your world intersects with someone on the inside of a company you are targeting. If you can find that, you will likely be one to three people removed from that person; that is a gap you can close.

Since we have been discussing Google you need to apply the principles of search when networking. The best way to find a needle in a haystack is to have a magnet. The magnet in networking is that person who will help open doors. What is it about you that will help them open the door for you?

Characteristics of a Good Networker

You have just finished reading about the importance of having a productive network that will fuel your job search. You have been given tools and techniques that will help you build a strong network. According to Dr. Ivan Misner and a study conducted by the Referral Institute, good networkers possess the following attributes.[27]

1. Enjoys helping others
2. Is Trustworthy
3. Works his or her network effectively
4. Follows up on referrals
5. Is a good listener

These attributes are listed in the order of the findings. Enjoys helping others is the number one attribute of a good networker and so on. While 'follows up on referrals' ranks fourth, I want to mention something that is obvious yet often overlooked. The reason you have a network is to find referrals. From my own personal experience I have given referrals and they have not been followed up. <u>The quickest way to kill a network is to not follow up on referrals you receive.</u> Following up on referrals is what leads to a job interview, which is the subject of our next chapter.

Remember information alone will not determine if you are a good networker. It is what you will do with it that matters.

Launch Checklist

Mission Readiness	Go	No Go
I have a clear understanding of how to build a productive network.		
I understand how to use social media in my networking efforts		
I am ready to put the tools I learned in this chapter to work.		
I am committed to be a good networker.		

Chapter 7

Selling Your Story Like Your Career Depends On It

> The story of the human race is the story of men and women selling themselves short.
> - Abraham Maslow, American Psychologist

An elevator pitch is the most powerful element in job search. It is the twenty-second commercial message that either results in a sale or the person turning the channel. This chapter builds on Chapter 3 by guiding you through a process to market your story that captures the imagination and interest of the listener--in less than a minute.

The Sell

I gave you great information in Chapter 2 on the importance of knowing your story and showed you how to write your story and communicate it through a compelling resume. I showed you how to use this story to create a 30-second infomercial called an elevator pitch that would capture the imagination and interest of people.

In the preceding chapter, I showed you how to use your story to build a productive network. In this chapter, I will take your story to next level and show you how to sell your story as though your career depended on it.

Your resume and elevator pitch are just the horderves to this amazing dinner. You may have attended functions where you filled up on the horderves and weren't hungry for the main course. In job search, that is not a problem because recruiters won't stop with your resume and elevator pitch. Those only peak their appetite for the main course.

The idea of selling your story may have a negative connotation. Whenever I think of sales I typically think of someone trying to sell me something I don't want to buy. But, selling your story is different. You are marketing and promoting your story to someone who wants to purchase but needs to be convinced before committing to the sale. Most of us are not natural salespeople especially when it comes to promoting ourselves. As you continue to read you will learn how to sell your story without feeling being self-conscious or a self-promoter. But first you need to conquer your fears.

Conquer Your Fears

Let me offer a personal story involving selling. Immediately after I graduated from college I had some job interviews lined up, but there was nothing I wanted to accept, so I took a position for the summer as a direct sales associate (otherwise known as a door-to-door salesperson). It was an opportunity to make some money and gain confidence.

The company was Southwestern Publishing Company, which was out of Nashville Tennessee. My sales territory was rural Kentucky. To successfully sell door to door, you need to first get into the potential customer's home. After attending a week of sales training I had mastered the art of getting invited into a person's house.

First, you knock on the door. Then you greet the person who answers with a statement that is disarming. My opening line was: "I'm just another pesky salesman...you don't shoot them do you?" (Of course, this line might not be appropriate today.) I would then hesitate and start wiping my feet on the doormat (even if they did not have one) to signal I was ready to enter. On my first day I was invited into the homes of 29 out of the 30 doors I knocked on. This was a phenomenal conversion rate, and that's the good news. The bad news is I did not make a sale, nothing, nada. Not even a little bit.

"No problem," the company had told us during training. If we continue getting into houses, the law of averages would eventually take over and we would make sales. I sold nothing the second day, and on the third day I found walking up to houses more and more difficult to the point that I eventually stopped. I sat in my car, paralyzed with fear.

Of course, our sales training had prepared us for this as well. We were to "do the thing you fear and that will be the end of fear." It was actually great advice, and they were right. Except, my fear was meeting strangers and I achieved that on my first day; but, now I faced a new fear – the fear of not selling.

You see, the law of averages is a belief that something will occur, not a mathematical probability that it will. If you flip a coin, there is a 50% chance that it will land on heads or tails regardless of the result of the previous flip. It did not take me long to rationalize that door-to-door sales were not for me. I lasted a total of two weeks -- but I did learn a valuable lesson.

I learned that I would continue to face circumstances and situations in life that would produce fear. Some of those circumstances, like impending danger, we need to heed. However, when fear threatens to limit your personal or professional growth, you need to do the thing you fear and that will be the end of it. The law of averages may not be a mathematical probability, but there is more likelihood you will land a job if you continue your job search activities than if you stop or short circuit them.

Selling is Easier than You Think

You may have heard of Hersey and Blanchard's Situational Leadership Theory or Situational Leadership Theory. Hersey and Blanchard identified four leadership styles that leader's use based on the readiness of followers. They identified four leadership styles, which are telling, selling, participating, and delegating.

I wrote my doctoral dissertation based on Hersey and Blanchard's Situational Leadership Theory (SLT). I studied professionals and executives at all levels within a Fortune 100 company. Without boring you with the details, I tested SLT and found that leaders, regardless of their level, tended to use two dominant leadership styles despite the readiness of the follower. The two styles were telling and selling.

The findings were consistent with my own personal leadership style. (You can take an assessment to determine your own situation leadership style.) Even though leaders adapt to the situation their dominant/default leadership style is telling and selling. While my study was a scientific study it does not mean the results are universal. However, I believe they are largely representative of most people. I know it is true for me and mostly you.

What does this have to do with job search? I will tell you. (Pun intended.) It means that telling and selling your story is something you are well equipped to do. In fact, it will come naturally to you, but you need to be aware how telling and selling works. Let me give you a non-job search example.

I am a pizza lover. I know I am not alone and there are lots of people who love pizza. So telling you I love pizza may not be enough to convince you that I am an exceptional pizza lover. So, you might want to know how many times a week I have pizza.

Before I got married it was at least three times a week, and after marriage it has been at least once a week. Our routine for over 30 years has been to have pizza every Friday night. But, having pizza weekly with my wife is not enough to convince you I am a pizza lover. So, you may need to hear more.

Perhaps this might help. Everywhere we have lived we have found a favorite place for pizza. We sometimes eat at the restaurant, but when I call for pick up and say I would like to order a pizza I am greeted with: "Hi Tom, the usual, meatball and mushroom?" "YES!" I respond enthusiastically.

Still not convinced? When we moved to California from the East Coast we told everyone we were moving including the owner of my favorite pizza restaurant. I had been going to his restaurant ever since I could drive. We were in California a year before we got back to the East Coast and I could stop in for my sausage pizza. When I greeted the owner Mr. Gervasio, he said to me "where have you been, I haven't seen you in a while?" I had to remind him we had moved to another State.

I think by now you are ordering Domino's and I have convinced you that I love pizza—if not, I have more. There's the time I had genuine New York Style pizza in Fairbanks, Alaska. I've got over 30 years of pizza stories. If you can have this much passion about pizza, imagine what you can do with the stories that really matter. By the way, Howard Schultz of Starbucks is just as excited about a coffee bean.

My face lights up when I talk to other people about pizza. That is what selling is all about. It is an unrehearsed emotion that demonstrates your passion and enthusiasm for something. It is the real you. That's what a recruiter and an interviewer want to see.

Seeking the Opportunity

Like some of you, I have attended networking functions, book signings, conferences, etc., where I got a chance to meet some "movers and shakers." I have stood in line waiting to shake their hand and sometimes pose for a photo. You have little time to say much of anything except smile, shake hands, say hello or nice to meet you, I am a big fan, I enjoyed your book or movie, and then you move on. These encounters are not designed to engage in a meaningful discussion. However, sometimes you find yourself in the right place at the right time with the right person. When that happens, are you prepared to tell your story?

I recently read Frances Hesselbein's book entitled *My Life in Leadership*. Prior to finding this book in my local library, I had no idea who Frances Hesselbein was. It turns out she is a former CEO of the Girls Scouts of America. She was the first CEO that came from the rank and file. She also received the Presidential

Medal of Freedom awarded to her by President Clinton. So, despite my limited knowledge, Frances had done quite well without me knowing her.

At the publication of this book, Frances is presently the President and CEO of the Leader to Leader Institute, formerly the Peter F. Drucker Foundation for Nonprofit Management. I was curious to learn how Frances became involved with Peter Drucker. For you none-business types, Peter Drucker invented the management principle of managing by objectives. He passed away in 2005, and many refer to him as a "management guru." One of his famous quotes is the best way to predict your future is to create it.

In Frances's book she writes:

> "The first day I walked into the office (as Executive Director Talus Rock Girl Scout Council), under my arm were six copies of Peter Drucker's *The Effective Executive*, one for each staff member. I did not know Peter Drucker..."

Frances became a big fan and follower of Drucker's work and implemented many of his ideas. Fast forward eleven years, Frances was invited to an event at which Peter Drucker was the featured speaker. The dinner included a 5:30 pm reception.

Frances arrived promptly at 5:30 pm, and the only people there were two bartenders. However, this changed a few seconds later when a man walked in. That's right, the man was Peter Drucker. He introduced himself to Frances who blurted out: "Do you know how important you are to the Girl Scouts?" To which he replied, "No, tell me." And she did. It was that chance encounter that led to a lasting friendship and professional relationship.

I know some of you think this could never happen to you. However, I believe this happens quite often. The difference is that Frances was prepared for a chance encounter. Are you?

Tips to Selling Your Story

Some tips to help you with selling your story.

1. **Your resume will not sell itself.** I think of courtrooms where lawyers often say the evidence speaks for itself. Not

true; the evidence may point in a certain direction but someone needs to connect the dots. Your resume is your story, and no one can tell your story better than you.

2. **The best sales people know their product.** We have all walked away from a purchase when a salesperson could not answer our questions about the product. In job search, you are the product. You should be able to answer with confidence and assurance any question a recruiter might have. Chapter 8 will show you how you can be sure.

3. **You can only sell if you yourself are convinced.**[28] Many job seekers make the mistake of trying to show interest in a job that they have no interest in. They think they can fake it, but the only person they are fooling is themselves. Bank tellers can tell counterfeit bills because they know how the real thing looks and feels. The same is true for recruiters. They can tell phony passion because real passion is genuine and credible.

4. **Keep selling until you make the sale.** A problem I have with selling is asking for the sale. I am afraid the answer will be no. However, a real salesperson wants to know even if the answer is no. They can then move on to the next person. One caution is that too much or too little selling can result in no sale. I have found that people will give you signals of when they have heard enough.

5. **Use social media to research the people you will meet.** In job search you will not always know in advance the people you will be meeting. However, if you do, you need to try and learn everything you can about them. This is part of your social media strategy (LinkedIn, Facebook, Twitter, etc.) discussed in Chapter 6 and will play an important part in selling your story.

6. **There is a buyer for every story.** This is not about the law of averages, but it is about the need to keep knocking on doors.

You have just completed part one of job search sales training. You have learned how to conquer your fears and sell your story with passion. You are now ready for part two of job search sales training and that is how to prepare for the ultimate sales test - a job interview.

Launch Checklist

Mission Readiness	Go	No Go
I will not let fear paralyze me in my job search.		
I am ready to tell and sell my story to anyone who will listen.		

Chapter 8

The Interview Before You Even Talk

"Give me six hours to chop down a tree and I will spend the first four sharpening the axe."
— Abraham Lincoln

The majority of job seekers are unprepared for a job interview. This chapter will show you how to prepare for an interview with confidence and the assurance to effectively answer any of the thousands of possible questions that could be asked.

Sitting on "The" Couch

I never dreamed I would be sitting on the couch of *The Tonight Show*. But, there I was on the couch, as our employees were entering the studio. My boss was hosting an All Employee Meeting and I was part of the agenda. What a setting! There is nothing like it. If only Jay was going to interview me. Thankfully, he was preparing for his show. But, what if he wasn't and I was one of his guests? Would I trip as I walked out on stage? Would I miss his hand during a handshake, or worse yet would my palms be wet? Would I perspire under the studio lights? Would I stammer in my responses? Would my mind go blank? Would my body shake?

Approximately six years prior I was working in Miami for NBC's television station WTVJ when I was sent to Burbank California to assist NBC employees in their recovery from the January 1994 Northridge Earthquake. I was asked to go because in August 1992 I was involved in helping WTVJ employees recover from Hurricane Andrew a Category 5 hurricane and among the top five costliest hurricanes.

While I was in Burbank I was asked if there was anything I wanted to see or do. They showed me damage the earthquake had caused on the production set of the *Fresh Prince of Bel-Air* (starring Will Smith), where fortunately no one was hurt. I asked if I could meet Jay Leno. I wanted to thank him on behalf of WTVJ employees for his generous contribution to a recovery fund that had been established following Hurricane Andrew.

A meeting was arranged, and I was ushered into a small office where Jay was standing behind his desk along with his assistant. I was introduced and Jay had his head down. After the brief intro I immediately said "I want to thank you on behalf of WTVJ employees for the assistance you provided in their recovery from Hurricane Andrew." He immediately lifted his head and looked and nodded his head in acknowledge, shook my hand and out the door I went. The whole meeting took less than a minute. I was able to say what I came prepared to say and it was effective. Let me repeat that. I was able to say what I came PREPARED to say and it was EFFECTIVE.

I have had the pleasure and privilege of meeting celebrities including the President of the United States. Some of these meetings were impromptu and others I knew about in advance. Regardless the encounter, the key to any meeting is preparation.

Preparation is the Key

If you ask someone who is about to be interviewed for a job if he or she is prepared, the answer will probably be 'yes'. But if you then ask them how he or she prepared, you will likely receive a variety of responses, including:

- I reviewed my resume
- I researched the company
- I bought a new suit
- I prepared responses to anticipated questions
- I had a friend ask me questions
- I used Google to create a list of good interview questions

Some of these methods may work; others, not so much. The problem most people have regarding preparing for job interviews is they do not know where to start. At the time this book was published, Google had 45 million results for 'Tips on Job Interviews," and bing.com had 32 million. There are so many resources available for job applicants that it can be overwhelming. I hope this chapter will simplify it a bit. Actually, I trust it simplifies it a lot.

For me, it starts with the basics, the very foundation that resulted in you being invited to interview in the first place. And contrary to popular belief, the interviewer will not just ask you about the content in your resume. This is because your resume will not address every aspect of the job or position description. A skilled interviewer will know how to mine for the additional information he or she needs – information that might not be on your resume. Pre-planning for the interview will go a long way to ensuring that you cover the important aspects of the position description, describing how your qualifications and experience match the company's needs, and even offer information that the interviewer hadn't thought to ask but can win you points.

Think of your resume and the position description providing you with the script you need to prepare for a job interview. A new suit might help; just remember to cut the tag off the sleeve. I forgot to do that once.

In the remaining sections I will explain some of the realities of the job interview process and show you how to turn opportunities into successes.

The Interview Process Reality Check

A major mistake that most job seekers make is going into an interview unprepared. Most job seekers get their interview training while on the job interview itself. This is not where you want to learn about interviewing. I know we spent a chapter on selling your story, and unfortunately that is where most job seekers will focus...and stop. But you can sell better if you are prepared and know your product—which is you.

You can achieve a competitive advantage over the competition if you just prepare for the interview. My goal in this chapter is to take the mystery and guesswork out of preparing for a job interview. Of course, it is impossible to know every question that you will be asked, but I will give some of the questions you can anticipate being asked and guide you on how to prepare your responses. While it is impossible to know what you will be asked, it IS POSSIBLE to be prepared to respond. Let's get started.

Preconceived Ideas about Interviewing

An impressive resume is the most important aspect to getting a job. This is an important aspect but not the most important. You still need to show how you achieved the accomplishments and then convince someone you are capable of doing the same and more for the company.

The candidate with the most experience and skill will get the job. Recall the times you have heard it said you are over qualified.

To an interviewer, a candidate's success in a previous job is a predictor of future success. The probability for future success based on past success is good but not 100%.

An interviewer who does most of the talking is interested in you and is trying to sell you on the job. There is some truth to this. I had a boss who did this and he hired some really great people. However, he was also good at assessing talent and did not hire everyone he interviewed.

Most interviewers are highly skilled in interviewing techniques. I estimate that less than 5% of the people who will interview you have received any kind of formal training on how to conduct an interview. This includes recruiters and human resource professionals.

Interviewers like to know that candidates have impressive references. I worked in the entertainment industry where everyone had impressive references. The best reference is the person who referred you.

Connecting with the interviewer on a personal level will make up for any lack of experience. You can turn on the personality all you want and leave the interview having made a new friend, but it doesn't me you will land the job.

Watching the "What Not to Wear" reality TV show can provide helpful tips on what to wear and not wear to an interview. Too bad this show is off the air because they did have some helpful hints. Maybe you can catch the reruns.

    These are but a few of the preconceived ideas that people may have about job interviewing. I share them to show that there is an opportunity for you to take control of the interview process. My goal is to have you be the best prepared candidate for the job interview and to help you overcome some of the inherent challenges of the interview process. As a job seeker you will spend the majority of your time trying to land a job interview, and once you do I want you to maximize the opportunity and hit the ball out of the ballpark.

    Consider a baseball metaphor. Every baseball player steps into the batter's box looking for a pitch he can hit. Preferably a fast ball. A smart pitcher knows this so he throws sliders and off speed pitches to mess with his timing. The pitcher then finishes him off with a high fast ball. This scenario changes when the batter is prepared to hit whatever pitch is thrown. This takes lots of batting practice. It takes a lot of practice preparing for a job interview.

    Once you are ready, you step into the interview box and:

1. **Be ready to swing at the first pitch.** The number one question asked 99.9% of the time is "tell me about yourself or some variation." This is the baseball equivalent of a soft ball. I have watched most job candidates take a half-hearted swing at this question. Most people don't think it is a serious question and for some interviewers it is not. However, when asked by a skilled interviewer it can mean the difference between landing a job and losing it.
2. **Make the job interviewer throw strikes.** It is easy for an interviewer to get off track and talk about the job and not ask specific questions. It is your job to make sure you do not leave an interview without the interviewee knowing how your qualifications match his or her needs.
3. **Be patient and aggressive.** While a job interview is a series of questions, there are some questions you can really drive. Make sure you do. What are those questions? Here's one: "Your accomplishments are great, now tell me how you did them."
4. **Be prepared for every type of question.** In baseball a great hitter is only great one-third of the time. This means the pitcher wins two-thirds of the time. The odds of you getting a hit at the right time improve when you can hit whatever pitch is thrown.

Most hiring managers are trying to strike you out. You can be ready but it takes practice.

Interviewing 101

Before the Interview

From the moment you first stepped into the prospective employer's office, your interview has already begun. The following are some important guidelines to keep in mind – before you even open your mouth.

- Know the correct pronunciation of the interviewer's name
- Arrive a few minutes early to the interview
- Bringing a notepad and a pen/pencil to take notes

- Always dress professionally – no matter what type of job you interview for
- Do not chew gum
- Turn off your cell phone

Common Interview Questions

There are two types of interview questions: general or behavioral. I will give you examples of both. You can prepare answers in advance for most general questions and behavioral questions. The general questions are fairly standard and widely known, which is one reason people don't prepare responses in advance. They think they know the answer. I advocate you prepare thoughtful responses.

Behavioral questions follow a format that is fairly standard, and once you understand you can prepare answers in advance. It is likely you will encounter a combination of these questions during the interview process. If you are being interviewed by more than one person it is likely each will ask you one or more of the same questions. By having prepared responses you can give the same response. Many interviewees think they need a different answer to the same question if asked it more than once. If you want people interviewing you to remember you and know the important aspects about your skills and abilities you need to be consistent in your responses. This may seem counterintuitive, but interviewers compare notes.

By knowing or understanding the questions in advance you can take the guesswork out of the interview process. This gives you more control of the outcome. You can count on being asked during a job interview one or more of the following questions or a variation.

General Questions

Tell me about yourself...*(This question/request is so important that it has its own detailed section later in this chapter.)*

What are your career goals? Your goals should be in 3 to 5 years. Something shorter signals you don't think the job you are interviewing for is that challenging or will hold your interest. Your goals should also be something that can be achieved in the organization where you are interviewing.

Why do you want to work here? This is an opportunity to show what you know about this company and the roles and responsibilities of the job (based on your research) and how it fits/matches your personal and professional goals and objectives.

What are your strengths/weaknesses? Since you have completed the Strengthsfinder Assessment, choose one of your strengths that best matches one of the job criteria. Be ready with more. Any strength that is overused can become a weakness. For example, I am a learner, which means I am curious about a lot of things and can ask a lot of questions and can keep asking questions. At some point you have to stop and make a decision. We all have weaknesses, but you should have a track record that shows they don't get in the way of results. I had a friend that was asked during an interview to give at least 5 weaknesses and if she couldn't she would not get the job. She rattled them off without hesitation. Most people try to dance around this question but if you address this head-on it might be refreshing. By the way she got the job.

Do you have any questions for me? I like to respond to this question by asking the interviewer if there is any concern about my ability to do the job that I need to address further. Most interviewers will tell you if they have any concerns. It lets you know where you stand. Other questions to consider might be: What keeps you up at night? I suggest that you have 2 or 3 questions and don't be afraid to ask the same question to different people. Going back to my example of being interviewed by Jay Leno, he does not ask each guest the same question because each guest has something different about him or her. He has some background on the guests and asks them about this associated with why they are there. For more, see the section in this chapter on "it's your turn to ask questions."

Behavioral Based Questions

Behavioral-based interview questions are among my favorite questions to ask. They are easy to recognize because they start with the word "tell, give, what or how". For example:

Tell *me about the most creative project you've worked on.* The operative word is "tell" and be specific. Another example could be "**tell** me about a project where you were the lead or a project that failed, etc." The person is being asked to recall a specific situation. **Tell** me about a time when you had to overcome obstacles to get the job done. Tell me about a time when you had to adapt quickly to a change. ***Give*** *me a specific example of a time when you took the initiative.*

What did you do? **How** did you do it? **What** were the outcomes? **What** did you learn? You may have heard the devil is in the details; behavioral-based questions let you get into the details without getting bogged down by them. To prepare for these questions you need to review your achievements and accomplishments. What is significant about those accomplishments as they relate to the requirements of the job? If the job posting/description is seeking experience in "x, y and z" then what in your experience matches that, and can you give me a specific example of the how and the what?

Below are a few examples taken from jobs posted on indeed.com.

Marketing Manager - Seeking someone to develop effective sales strategies that cater to multiple touch points at prospective clients (e.g., user of the service and decision maker may often be different—ability to foster buy-in from all constituencies).

Examples of Behavioral Questions: Give me an example of when you developed a sales strategy that catered to multiple clients? What did you do? What was the outcome?

Chief Information Officer - Align IT objectives and programs with the organizations overall vision, strategies and objectives.

Examples of Behavioral Questions: Give me an example of how you have aligned IT programs with the strategies and objectives of the business? What did you do? What specific challenges did you have to overcome? What was the outcome?

<u>Financial Analyst</u> - Assist in development of forward-looking financial plans, including budgets, forecasts and long-range financial plans

Examples of Behavioral Questions: Give me an example of a project you've worked on involving long-range financial plans? What did you do? What was the outcome?

I trust you can see that behavioral questions follow a similar format regardless of the job. You just need to figure out examples in your background that can address the "tell, give, what and how." With a little advance planning you will be able to extract significant examples from your background and sell that during an interview. If you try to recall it "ad hoc" you may get the wrong story.

It's Your Turn to Ask Questions

Willa Plank wrote in the *Wall Street Journal* an article about the *Five Must Ask Interview Questions*.[29] She interviewed Ben Dattner of Dattner Consulting to get his advice on what interview questions an employer should ask a candidate to assure they hire wisely. I thought these were apropos to share with you, and it would serve you well to think about them and prepare responses to each. The five questions are as follows:

1. In what ways will this role help you stretch your professional capabilities?
2. What have been your greatest areas of improvement in your career?
3. What's the toughest feedback you've ever received and how did you learn from it?
4. What are people likely to misunderstand about you?

5. If you were giving your new staff a "user's manual" to you, to accelerate their "getting to know you" process, what would you include in it?

The goal in asking these questions, albeit cleverly worded, are designed to get you to divulge the "real you," your weaknesses and how you might fit in the organization. They are direct and will cause the inexperienced or seasoned job candidate to drop his or her guard and blurt out something unrehearsed. That is an interviewer's dream and the job candidate's potential nightmare.

However, consider a different perspective. Flip the questions around. Could you use these questions to get the interviewer to reveal the "real organization"? Imagine asking the following:

1. In what ways will this role keep me from stretching my professional capabilities?
2. What are the greatest areas of need for improvement in this organization?
3. What is the organization's experience with people who provide candid and direct feedback?
4. I imagine human behavior being what it is can result in misunderstandings. What has been the process of dealing with them?
5. If I am hired, what is the best way for me to accelerate my getting to know the team?
6. What is it about your job that is not as much fun or you don't like?

In order to determine whether you will fit in, you need to know the strengths and weaknesses of the organization just as much as they want to know yours. You have heard it said the best offense is a good defense. Well, I believe the best offense is a good offense.

How to Respond

I have given you examples of general and behavior-based interview questions. Next, you will need to learn how to prepare answers to these types of questions, starting with behavior-based questions.

Behavior Based Interview Questions:

Since acronyms can help us remember important information, two are particularly helpful when responding to behavior-based interview questions. They are STAR and SOAR. STAR stands for (Situation, Task, Action, Results), and SOAR (Situation, Opportunity, Action, Results). We will discuss Situation, Task/Opportunity, Action, and Results.

Situation
You need to recall recent situations that show favorable behaviors or actions, especially involving course work, work experience, leadership, teamwork, initiative, planning, and customer service. Be specific. Don't generalize about several events; give a detailed accounting of one event. Use your achievements and accomplishments from your resume as a reference point. These situations should closely match the needs the employer is seeking and referenced in the job posting/description.

Task/Opportunity
Then prepare a short description of each situation: the who, what, when, where and how -- and be ready to provide details.

Action
Be sure each situation/vignette/story has a beginning, a middle, and an end, i.e., be ready to describe the situation, your action, and the outcome or result. Be honest. Don't embellish or omit any part of the story. The interviewer will find out if your story is built on a weak foundation.

Results
Be sure the outcome or result reflects positively on you (even if the result itself was not favorable). Provide measureable results. Remember to quantify everything.

I want to emphasize that your resume is your story and that is what the interviewer has in front of him or her and is what they will use to probe your skills and abilities. Interviewers will seek to validate the information you have provided and assess whether your qualifications match their needs. Don't assume they will see the connection to your experiences. You need to sell your story by showing them specifically how you fit their needs. The more you can demonstrate how your achievements and accomplishments match, the better. And hopefully the interviewer will make notes. Make their job easy and do it for them.

The Most Frequently Asked Interview Question

Explaining complex issues is challenging because you need to figure out what to leave out. Try nothing. How do you do that? You will need to: Keep It Short and Straightforward [KISS].

In job interviews the number one most-asked question is the easiest. And yet ironically it is the toughest question. In fact, it's not a question, really. It's more like a statement. It is: "Tell me about yourself." It is easy because you know it is coming, and is usually one of the first questions asked, and yet most people don't know what you want to say.

The interviewer wants you to relax, so he or she offers up a softball question, which you should easily hit out of the ballpark, but it usually results in a slow hopper to the pitcher's mound. No harm; this was a throw away question, right, perhaps, but this missed opportunity and is strike one. However, if you have prepared your elevator pitch you have just circled the bases.

In all the interviews I have conducted the conversation generally goes like this.

> ***Me the interviewer***: "So, what can you tell me about yourself?"
>
> ***Interviewee:*** "Um, what do you want to know?"

If you want to WOW the interviewer, you need to be prepared with the right answer, and the right answer is your succinct, compelling, and well-rehearsed elevator pitch. Think about it. What is your passion, what difference have you made and how will you contribute in the future? And why should they care? Make them care with sharing a powerful story about your professional life. My mother calls me her most challenging child. Why's that I said. She had immediately captured my attention and interest.

Use action words that are believable and avoid self-aggrandizing statements. Memorize and rehearse your answer until it flows naturally and convincingly. That is what actors do. In this movie you get to play yourself. When you get your response down to 60 seconds then try reducing the scene to 15 memorable seconds. Impossible, really, then try two words. HOME RUN. *For more, review Chapter 3 about creating the perfect elevator pitch and then make sure you practice and use it.*

Behind the Curtain: How the Interviewer Prepares

While you are preparing for your job interview the recruiter is also preparing. The amount of preparation you will need to do should be much more than those who will interview you. It is helpful to know what exactly is happening on the hiring end. Below are some things an interviewer might do to prepare for an interview. It is important to know the information they are reviewing was provided by you.

Try to put yourself in their shoes. What would you want to know about you?

- Review the candidate's resume
- Check the candidate out on social media (LinkedIn, Facebook, etc.)
- Make note of any inconsistencies on the resume
- Make note of any accomplishments
- Match the candidate's experiences to the job requirements
- Determine what questions to ask about the candidate's qualifications
- Look for points of interest. This could be most anything from schools, a thesis, sororities, hobbies, volunteer groups, associations; places lived or worked, etc. These are

mostly human interest kinds of things but occasionally can result in something more significant. I had a student once who did his master's thesis on graffiti. Pretty interesting as there are some mathematic applications to it.

Interviewing Do's and Don'ts

The following do's and don'ts are by no means exhaustive, yet if you keep these in mind you will help you interview like a STAR and SOAR.

Do.........
- ✓ Research the Company
- ✓ Review recent press releases about the company and any items in the media and company news
- ✓ Learn the company structure (who reports to whom)
- ✓ NETWORK for perspectives on the business and the interviewers (use Google, LinkedIn, ZoomInfo)
- ✓ Make sure the information on your resume is correct
- ✓ Anticipate tough questions
- ✓ Practice, Practice, Practice...with a friend, in front of the mirror, formal mock interviews, etc.
- ✓ Develop stories and examples that highlight your accomplishments
- ✓ Treat EVERYONE in the process with respect
- ✓ BE FRIENDLY!!!
- ✓ ARRIVE EARLY!

Don't.........
- ✓ Be someone you're not. Be yourself. You will be far more successful if your abilities match your self-assessment output.
- ✓ Leave the interview without making sure you have communicated your interest in the job. Say it; don't assume they know.
- ✓ Leave the interview without asking key questions. If the job is a right fit for you, get the information you need to make the right decision. Things like what are the next steps. When do they expect to make a decision?

- ✓ Forget to write a thank-you note. Not only is this a professional courtesy, but it is an opportunity to mention some follow-up facts about your interest and qualifications based on any feedback to the question about do they have any concerns about your qualifications.
- ✓ Be too casual. Remember, you are interviewing for a professional position, so dress in business attire.

Low Self-Esteem – The Secret Weapon to Great Interviewing

Jay Leno is a great believer in low self-esteem. He says "if you don't think you're the smartest person in the room and you think you're going to have to work a little harder, and put a little more time into it, to get what everybody else does, you can actually do quite well. And that's been my approach."[30]

I began this chapter with the goal of taking the mystery and guesswork out of preparing for a job interview. I gave you a process for preparing your responses and showed you the tools to use in formulating your responses. You can now be confident that regardless what the interviewer throws you can hit it out of the park. All you need to do is put in the effort.

Launch Checklist

Mission Readiness	Go	No Go
I recognize the common misconceptions about job interviewing and will work to avoid them.		
I will practice the STAR or SOAR technique in preparing for an interview.		
I will prepare questions to ask the interviewer(s)		
I commit to having a solid response to the question tell me about yourself.		

Chapter 9

Careertography – Mapping a Winning Strategy

"Tactics Without a Strategy is Worse Than Doing Nothing at All"

– Li Evans

Now that you have the essential tools and techniques necessary to conduct a productive career search, it is time to implement a plan of action to achieve that end goal. This chapter shows you how to construct a winning career search strategy.

Start at the End and Work Backwards

This book began with step one: Create your story. You can now fast forward from the present to the end of your story, which is, of course, when you land that job you are passionate about. The end of your story will likely have an epilogue, but for the job search process we will start with the end and work backwards to construct your job search strategy. As you execute your strategy you will use the tactics discussed in the book, such as an elevator pitch, a compelling resume, building a network and strong interview skills.

Job Search Strategy

STEP ONE (which is THE END): Determine the job that has passion and purpose

STEP TWO: Match your skills to job requirements

STEP THREE: Target the companies that have the job that has passion and purpose

STEP FOUR: Work your network to open doors to the companies that have the job that speaks most to your passions

STEP FIVE: Work your strategy until you achieve THE END

Assessing Your Chances

In Chapter 2, I mentioned that one of the common mistakes job seekers make is not focusing on the 80/20 rule. The 80/20 rule is where employers are seeking candidates that match at least 80% of their job requirements. Figure 1 is a simple decision tree that you can use to help determine in advance if you meet the 80% threshold.

The decision starts with the job you are considering. I recommend you evaluate each individual requirement separately. This enables you to not only assess your skills and experience but also to identify any gaps and determine whether they are significant and how you might close them.

You assess each category where green means you match at least 80% of that requirement, yellow means you match at least 50% and red means you match at least 25% or less of the requirement. After you evaluate each category, you total all 5 categories (your strengths, work experience, achievements, education and other criteria) and the maximum that can be achieved 4.0. You need to achieve at least 3.2 to match 80% of the job requirements.

Each category in the Decision Tree has the same value (or weight). However, as you use the tree you should weight the categories based on the job requirements. Also, this assessment includes your strengths, which may or may not be on your resume. I include them because they will be a major factor when interviewing.

Figure 1: Decision Tree to Assess 80/20 Rule

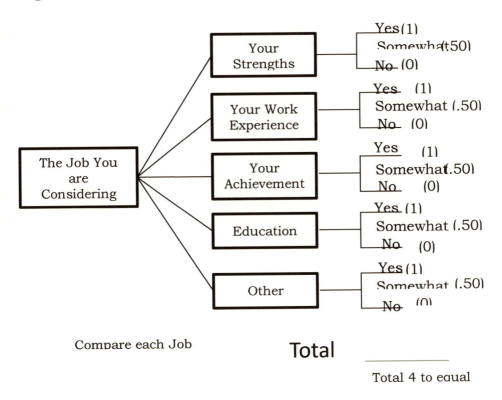

Compare each Job

Total _____

Total 4 to equal

You can adapt this tree to assess the strength of your network (see Figure 2). These tools can help you be more objective when evaluating your job qualifications and network.

Figure 2: Decision Tree to Assess the Strength of Your Network

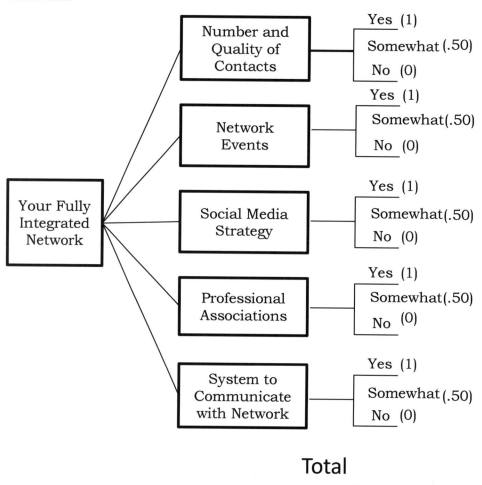

Monitoring Your Progress

It is a lot of work preparing for and conducting a job search. Once you are fully engaged in job search you need to continuously assess the effectiveness of your job search. Figure 3 is a dashboard you can use to evaluate how well your job search strategy and tactics are working.

Evaluate the effectiveness of your resume by the feedback you receive from recruiters and hopefully job interviews. This will indicate whether you need to make any adjustments or changes.

Evaluate your network by the number of referrals you are receiving. You evaluate your interviewing by the feedback you receive from recruiters and/or hiring managers.

Every job search requires adaptation. By using the decision trees and dashboard you will be able to identify areas where you need to improve your job search strategy, resume, interviewing, and networking. It can also build your confidence and motivate you.

Figure 3. Job Search Dashboard

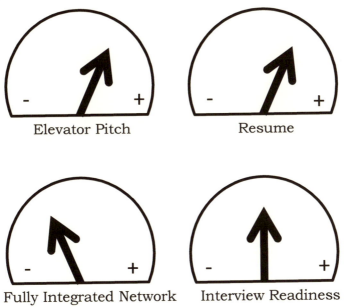

Launch Checklist

Mission Readiness	Go	No Go
I will prepare a job search strategy and then execute it using the tactics I have learned in this book.		
I will use a decision tree to assess my qualifications for potential jobs.		
I will use a decision tree to help improve the effectiveness of my network		
I will monitor my job search strategy and make adjustments when necessary.		

Chapter 10

Catching the Ideal Career Search Wave

This chapter will encourage you to launch your career search by identifying the various waves of employment activity that typically occur in a career search. Similar to a surfer seeking that perfect wave, the job seeker must recognize (and seize!) the opportunities and then act accordingly.

Review the Checklist

My goal in writing this book was to cut through the mystery and guesswork of job search "how tos" and focus on the essential ingredients to finding and landing a career/job that matches your skills, goals and passion. I wanted to give you practical and easy-to-do tools and show you how to apply them in your job search to achieve your desired outcome. The purpose of this final chapter is to review the checklist one last time, reflect on the journey ahead and get started for the ride of a lifetime.

I used to love flying, but one rough flight from Dallas to San Antonio in a thunder storm turned me into a white knuckle flyer. I had flown a lot after that flight but was always anxious until we landed. When I was working for NBC, I had the opportunity to fly in a private jet.. On this particular flight my boss and colleagues decided to perform an intervention and put me in the jump seat. I sat between the pilot and the co-pilot. Fabulous view!

As the plane started down the runway there was no turning back. I had nowhere to go so I kept my eyes open and observed. Of course, everywhere in the back was watching me. As we raced down the runway there were several times I expected liftoff, but the pilot kept the plane on the ground. The operative word here is the pilot kept the plane on the ground.

After we took off and the plane reached an altitude where we could talk and I was quick to ask the pilot how he knew when to take off. He told me the toughest thing for a pilot is to keep the plane on the ground because the plane wants to fly. However, you can't experience liftoff until the time is right and the plane will stay up. I was not entirely cured, but ever since then I have less anxiety about flying.

You are the pilot of your job search. As you read this book I trust the toughest thing was keeping the plane on the ground until the right time. So, now is the time for the final review as you race down the runway preparing your story, creating your resume, weaving your network and practicing your interview skills to achieve your most fulfilling career.

Your mission SHOULD YOU CHOOSE TO ACCEPT IT is to review the following final status checklist to determine your readiness to launch a successful job search.

Mission Readiness	Go	No Go
Chapter 1: Do What You Love and Love What You Do		
I am ready to be one of the 30% who loves their job.		
I completed a Career Assessment		
I know my career passion and will pursue it		
Chapter 2: Mission Possible		
I set specific job search goals.		
I have a system to organize my job search efforts		
I plan to proactively target companies I am interested in		
I understand the 80/20 rule and will use it in my job search		
I will use whatever job search advice I believe will work for me		
I understand the role of executive recruiters in the job search process		
I know my job criteria and have a system to evaluate job opportunities		
I will safeguard and nurture my network.		
I will step outside my comfort zone.		
Chapter 3: Creating Your Competitive Advantage		
I reached deep into my autobiographical memory and recalled specific situations, experiences and events.		
I completed a Strengthsfinder 2.0 assessment		
I used the tools outlined in the chapter to create my mind map.		
I created an Elevator Pitch that communicates my passion, my capabilities and is unforgettable.		
Chapter 4: Hidden Truths For a Successful Career Search		
I know the three most important activities in job search.		
I understand why my story is the key to everything in job search.		
I understand I am living in a non-linear world.		
To increase my job prospects I must decrease them.		
I now know how to navigate Automated Tracking		

Systems.		
Chapter 5: The 8 Essential Ingredients of a Compelling Resume		
I know what I need to do to pass the 6 second test		
I will not write my resume without some professional help		
I will focus on how I can use the 8 essential ingredients to create my resume		
Chapter 6: Optimizing Your Network Channels		
I have a clear understanding of how to build a productive network.		
I understand how to use social media in my networking efforts		
I am ready to put the tools I learned in this chapter to work.		
I am committed to be a good networker.		
Chapter 7: Selling Your Story Like Your Career Depends On It		
I will not let fear paralyze me in my job search.		
I am ready to tell and sell my story to anyone who will listen.		
Chapter 8: The Interview Before You Even Talk		
I recognize the common misconceptions about job interviewing and will work to avoid them.		
I will practice the STAR or SOAR technique in preparing for an interview.		
I will prepare questions to ask the interviewer(s)		
I commit to having a solid response to the question tell me about yourself.		
Chapter 9: Careertography – Mapping a Winning Strategy		
I will prepare a job search strategy and then execute it using the tactics I have learned in this book.		
I will use a decision tree to assess my qualifications for potential jobs.		
I will use a decision tree to help improve the effectiveness of my network		
I will monitor my job search strategy and make adjustments when necessary.		

I recommend every item on the checklist be marked Go! However, I have italicized in the checklist select items that when marked Go will make a positive difference to you achieving your job search goals and objectives.

Rev Up Your Engine!

In the spirit of fun metaphors that can really illustrate the career search process, I thought it apropos to begin with the lyrics from the 1960s "Born to Be Wild" song by Steppenwolf:

Get your motor running,
Head out on the highway,
Looking for adventure,
And whatever comes our way.

I especially love the line later in the song:

Yeah, I got to go make it happen.

You may have heard it said that life is like a marathon that is run like a sprint. I have never run a marathon, but I have friends who have (I once trained for one!). You would be interested to know that when athletes train for a marathon, they rarely, if ever, run the complete 26 miles and 385 yards until the actual race day.

However, they still need to run a total of at least 40 miles a week for three or four months leading up to the race. Some who don't train that way will have a hard time completing the race. So, a marathon is really a series of small to medium-sized races.

Fun side note: The final 385 yards are more important than you might think. To learn why, check out the 1908 Olympic Marathon considered "the greatest race of the century."

Running a marathon is a good metaphor for one's career search. You need to target a time for when you want to land a job. However, the pace is different for every runner. You need to set a pace that is right for you and try to maintain it for the duration of the search process, but that does not mean you run at the same speed all the time.

In the career search, you need to be able to pick up the pace and/or slow the pace while maintaining a consistent pace.

Anyone who has served in the military is familiar with the phrase *hurry up and wait*. The same is true in job search. The process moves quickly in the beginning. Recruiters are calling, you are sending out resumes and returning calls, going to meet people and then like many marathon runners you hit The Wall.

The Wall in running is when the runner is depleted of glycogen, which is our source of energy. It attacks their muscles and they can't move their legs. It is physical. In job search it is emotional. Nothing can zap your energy more than no one getting back to you especially after sending a resume (at their request) or a referral or an interview. Self-doubt begins to creep in. It happens to everyone. You are not alone although you may feel alone.

You may think it is because you are not smart or qualified or your age or some other reason. Listen to me: none of these are true. It is because the right person has not seen your qualifications at the right time for the right job.

When runners hit the wall, it can be because the brain is telling the legs to move but the legs are drained of the nutrients they need to function. However, it can also be because the brain wants to quit and not tell the legs to move.

In job search, our body can still send out resumes, go to a networking meeting, send emails and make phone calls, but our mind may want to give up because no one is calling back. It is normal to expect results from our efforts. However, no results are results -- just not the results you want. When this happens it is not because you are not qualified or doing the right things. It is because your resume has not gotten to the person at the right time that has the right job for you.

A major part of being successful in sports and life is mental discipline. Mental discipline is more than not giving up. It is staying focused on the task. In job search, this is telling and selling your story, continuous networking and knocking on doors until the right one opens. Keep your job search running.

You Have the Controls

To continue my flying metaphor you have now been given the controls. You have completed the checklist and taxied to the runway and have taken off. You are in flight and when you encounter turbulence remember the following:

Make sure you have people cheering for you. Surround yourself with people who have your best interests and are a positive influence. Their words can greatly affect those already in your head.

React proactively. You have heard the saying "stuff happens"...well, it does. Make sure you are the person who makes things happen, and not vice-versa.

Finish the flight. Perseverance is responsible for more success than failure.

Don't Forget to Follow Up

This may shock you but many job seekers do not follow up on phone calls, emails, meetings, referrals or job interviews, etc. The following reasons are why you should follow up when job hunting.[31]

Reason #1: This is a chance for you to set yourself apart and be remembered. 75% of people do not send a thank you note even after a formal interview. Sometimes job seekers do not want to follow up because they don't want to be annoying. It is more annoying not to follow up.

Reason #2: It is necessary to developing good guanxi (pronounced gwan-shee). Relationships are critical to job search and life. I was introduced to the concept of Guanxi while traveling in China. In the Chinese culture guanxi stands for relationships where people support and cooperate with each other. Guanxi takes time and resources to develop. Once good guanxi is achieved it results in a free exchange of favors between the two. In job search too many job seekers think that relationship is one way and consequently do not invest in building strong relationships. The best relationships are two-way.

Reason #3: It's another opportunity to clarify or add new information. There is always something you wish you would have said or said differently. If it is significant a follow up is a good way to tie up loose ends.

All Systems Go

The year I started looking for my first "real" job, the unemployment rate was 7.8%. That was over 30 years ago and not much has changed. During those 30 years, the unemployment rate has fluctuated from a high of 10.8% to a low of 3.8%. It is tough and job search will always remain tough but if you're tenacious and persevere you will get a job offer.

I want to close this book my first thanking you for reading it. There are other books about job search you could have read or things you could have been doing so I thank you.

After college I was drafted into the Army, but I chose to enlist in the United States Air Force. The Air Force guaranteed me a job as a Personnel Specialist This enabled me to launch my career in human resource management although back then it was called Personnel and still is in some places today.

It was an honor and privilege to serve. Every three months we would gather for a townhall meeting with our superiors. We would be briefed on what was happening and the meeting would always end with a video entitled "Airforce Now." The video featured what the men and women of the Airforce were doing to achieve the mission, it showed the challenges and accomplishments and of course lots of planes flying. Close your eyes and imagine hearing the Airforce song with jet engines blazing:

> "Off we go into the wild blue yonder,
> Climbing high into the sun.
> Here they come zooming to meet
> our thunder At 'em boys,
> Give 'er the gun!
>
> Down we dive, spouting
> our flame from under
> Off with one helluva roar!
>
> We live in fame or
> go down in flame.
> Hey! Nothing can stop the U.S. Air Force!"

I still get goose bumps whenever I hear that song. By the time the video ended, we were holding back tears, standing tall and ready to conquer the world. I trust that is how you feel after reading this book and are ready to find and land that job and career that you desire most. All Systems Go!

In the words of Forest Gump, "that's all I have to say about that!"

Index

B

Branding yourself, 50

C

Career

    assessing interests, 39

    definition, 14

    developmental stages, 18

    transitioning, 20

Careertography, *128*

E

Elevator pitch

    definition, 48

    guidelines, 54

    importance, 48

    misconceptions, 49

Executive recruiters, 32

H

Hiring managers, 30

I

Interviewing, 112

    asking questions, 120

    common questions, 117

    do's and don'ts, *125*

    FAQ, *123*

    preparing, 113

    reality check, 114

    responding to questions, 122

J

Job

    definition, 14

    evaluating job criteria, 33

    loss, 26

    mirepoix, 60

    search mistakes, 27

    search process, 60

L

LinkedIn

   creating profile, 90

M

Mirepoix, 60

N

Network

   characteristics of good networker, 102

   common misconceptions, 85

   definition, 85

   growing, 34

   maximizing social networking, 92

   networking do's and don'ts, 94

   networking when employed, 98

   the who's who, 99

   why you need it, 84

P

Pitching your story, 104

   overcoming fears, 104

   seeking opportunities, 107

   tips for selling it, 108

R

Recruiters, 73

Resume

   8 essential ingredients, 72

   choosing resume writer, 68

   need for compelling story, 68

Retirement

   preparing, 38

S

Social media

   creating LinkedIn profile, 90

   maximizing network, 92

   optimizing job search, 88

Strengthsfinder, 47

Endnotes

[1] Werner, Jon. M. and Randy L. DeSimone Human Resource Development 6th Edition, p. 396

[2] Ibid., p. 402

[3] Bridges, William Transitions: Making Sense of Life's Changes Addison-Wesley Publications c1980

[4] Locke, Edwin A. Toward a Theory of Task Motivation and Incentives Organization Behavior and Human Performance Volume 3, Issue 2, May 1968, Pages 157–189

[5] Smith, Jacqueline 7 Things You Probably Didn't Know About Your Job Search, Forbes.com April 17, 2013 retrieved July 27, 2013

[6] Segall, Laurie Marissa Mayer: Yahoo gets 12,000 resumes a week, CNN Money.com September 11, 2013 http://money.cnn.com/2013/09/11/technology/marissa-mayer-yahoo-techcrunch/index.html?section=money_topstories&utm_source=feedburner&utm_medium=feed&utm_campaign=Feed%3A+rss%2Fmoney_topstories+(Top+Stories)

[7] Donlin, Kevin "How to Target Hiring Managers and Crack the Hidden Job Market Career Jockey April 14, 2010 http://careerjockey.org/how-to-target-hiring-managers-and-crack-the-hidden-job-market/

[8] SmartRecruiters.com Marketing Associate https://www.smartrecruiters.com/ReeherLLC/74012016-marketing-assoicate

[9] Proverbs 15:22 The Message

[10] Jacobs, Deborah L. Seven Things a Headhunter Won't Tell You Forbes.com July 26, 2012 http://www.forbes.com/sites/deborahljacobs/2012/07/26/7-things-a-headhunter-wont-tell-you/

[11] Worldwide ERC U.S. Domestic Transfers: Relocation Statistics 2013 http://www.worldwideerc.org/resources/research/pages/facts-and-statistics.aspx

[12] Americans Leaving the US in Record Numbers RT.com December 7, 2011 http://rt.com/usa/leaving-us-america-country-289/

[13] Nash Unsworth, Gregory J. Spillers & Gene A. Brewer (2012): The role of working memory capacity in autobiographical retrieval: Individual differences in strategic search, Memory, 20:2, 167-176

[14] (LinkedIn Says Most Overused Buzzwords Are "Extensive Experience, Innovative and Motivated", 2010)http://www.businesswire.com/news/home/20101214005059/en/LinkedIn-Overused-Buzzwords-%E2%80%9CExtensive-Experience-Innovative-Motivated%E2%80%9D

[15] Stone, Kay How to Craft a Killer Elevator Pitch that will Land You Big Business Dumblittleman.com August 1, 2007 http://www.dumblittleman.com/2007/08/how-to-craft-killer-elevator-pitch-that.html

[16] Squawkfox.com http://www.squawkfox.com/2008/06/09/how-to-match-your-skills-to-employer-requirements/

[17] The Ladders, Keeping an Eye on Recruiter Behavior http://cdn.theladders.net/static/images/basicSite/pdfs/TheLadders-EyeTracking-StudyC2.pdf Retreived August 8, 2013

[18] Ibid. page 4

[19] Womack, Brian Google Gets Record 75,000 Applications in a Week, Feb 3, 2011 http://www.bloomberg.com/news/2011-02-03/google-gets-75-000-job-applications-in-one-week-topping-record-set-in-07.html

[20] Change Your Words Change Your World Purplefeather.co.uk http://www.youtube.com/watch_popup?v=Hzgzim5m7oU&vq=medium

[21] Sterbenz, Christina 11 Common Grammatical Mistakes and How to Avoid Them BusinessInsider.com September 12, 2013 http://www.businessinsider.com/11-common-grammatical-mistakes-and-how-to-avoid-them-2013-9

[22] About Us: LinkedIn. January 31, 2014, http://www.linkedin.com/about-us

[23] Arruda, William "9 Reasons Why You Must Update Your LinkedIn Profile Today" Forbes.com November 25, 2013 http://www.forbes.com/sites/williamarruda/2013/11/25/9-reasons-why-you-must-update-your-linkedin-profile-today

[24] Finding and Joining a Group LinkedIn.com http://help.linkedin.com/app/answers/detail/a_id/186

arino, Lisa Do Good Feel Good, MSN Healthy Living http://healthyliving.msn.com/diseases/depression/do-good-feel-good-1

26 eBizMBA Top 15 Most Popular Job Websites August 2013 http://www.ebizmba.com/articles/job-websites

27 Misner, Ivan Top Traits of a Good Networker Business Networking with Dr. Ivan Misner May 3, 2010 http://businessnetworking.com/traits-of-a-good-networker/

28 Szaky, Tom My Top Ten Sales Tips The New York Times July 25, 2011 http://boss.blogs.nytimes.com/2011/07/25/my-top-10-sales-tips/?_r=0

29 Plank, Willa "Five Must Ask Interview Questions" Wall Street Journal April 29, 2010 http://online.wsj.com/article/SB10001424052748704302304575213962794390050.html

30 Crockett, Kathy Jay Leno The Yale Center for Dyslexia and Creativity http://dyslexia.yale.edu/leno.html

31 Urschel, Harry Follow Up, Follow Up, Follow Up!!! Career Rocketeer May 14, 2010 http://careerrocketeer.com/2010/05/follow-up-follow-up-follow-up.html

ABOUT TOM CAIRNS

Fulbright Scholar and Associate Professor School of Business and Management, Azusa Pacific University, California. Former Senior VP Human Resources NBC Universal and former Presidential Appointee as Chief Human Capital Officer US Department Homeland Security.

Dr. Tom Cairns has lead large complex and dynamic human resource management organizations. He is acknowledged for creating and staffing complex organizations in high performance cultures that consistently delivered business results. Tom has assisted hundreds of professionals at all levels to achieve their career goals and objectives.